HIDDEN RUNWAYS

HIDDEN RUNWAYS

LEN CURRERI

Library Tales Publishing

Library Tales Publishing

www.LibraryTalesPublishing.com

Copyright © 2025 by Len Curerri

All Rights Reserved

Published in New York, New York.

No part of this publication may be reproduced, stored in a retrieval system, or transmitted in any form or by any means, electronic, mechanical, photocopying, recording, scanning, or otherwise, except as permitted under Sections 107 or 108 of the 1976 United States Copyright Act, without the prior written permission of the Publisher. Requests to the Publisher for permission should be addressed to the Legal Department: Legal@LibraryTales.com

Trademarks: Library Tales Publishing, Library Tales, the Library Tales Publishing logo, and related trade dress are trademarks or registered trademarks of Library Tales Publishing and/or its affiliates in the United States and other countries, and may not be used without written permission. All other trademarks are the property of their respective owners.

For general information on our other products and services, please contact our Customer Care Department at 1-800-754-5016, or fax 917-463-0892. For technical support, please visit www.LibraryTalesPublishing.com

Library Tales Publishing also publishes its books in a variety of electronic formats. Every content that appears in print is available in electronic books.

9798894410364

Printed in the United States of America

CONTENTS

Disclaimer	vii
Dedication	ix
Curreri Air	xiii
Introduction	xv
Preface	xxv
1. Flight 01L	1
2. Flight 02R	6
3. Flight 03L	13
4. Flight 04R	16
5. Flight 05L	23
6. Flight 06R	27
7. Flight 07L	30
8. Flight 08R	37
9. Flight 09L	48
10. Flight 10R	52
11. Flight 11L	54
12. FLIGHT 12R Corporate Flight Operations	59
13. Flight 13L	62
14. Flight 14R	64
15. Flight 15L	67
16. Flight 16R	71
17. Hidden Runway 17L	79
18. Flight 18R	82
19. Flight 19L	85
20. Flight 20R	87
21. Flight 21L	91
22. Hidden Runway 22R	97
23. Flight 23L	100
24. Flight 24R	109
25. Flight 25L	113
26. Flight 26R	116
27. Flight 27L	123
28. Flight 28R	127
29. Flight 29L	130

30. Flight 30R	133
31. Flight 31L	137
32. Lastly, a Few Words of Wisdom from Jimmy Buffett	143
33. The End!	145
Acknowledgments	147

DISCLAIMER

Disclaimer: Many of the references in this book are personal friends or close acquaintances, all of whom I consider part of my "extended family." This book gave me the opportunity to honor and express my gratitude for their invaluable contributions to the success of my career and life. The photographs included in this book were personally generated by me, and I have obtained permission to use pictures taken by named third parties with credit associated with the still images or video. To respect privacy, some individuals are identified only by their first name and the initial of their last name.

DEDICATION

The world changed forever with the passing of Jimmy Buffett on September 1, 2023. His vibrant spirit, music, and unyielding zest for life left an indelible mark, not only on the millions who adored him but also on those lucky enough to know him personally. I count myself among that fortunate few. The moments I shared with Jimmy stand as some of the most cherished in my life. I was privileged to fly alongside him, immersing myself in the magic of the Margaritaville family—a community brimming with joy, creativity, and a sense of belonging.

After my time with Jimmy, I embarked on a new chapter as a freelance contract pilot. This transition broadened my horizons, both literally and figuratively. It opened the door to extraordinary opportunities, allowing me to navigate diverse flight operations and discover remote runways tucked away in corners of the world I might never have otherwise explored. Each journey brought with it a unique set of challenges and rewards, enriching my life and career in ways I could never have imagined.

None of this incredible journey would have been possible without the unwavering support of my wife, Elli. While I was crisscrossing the globe, Elli was the anchor that kept our family grounded. She raised and cared for our children, Cristina and Marc, ensuring that despite my frequent absences, our lives remained steady and full of love. Her strength, faith, and dedication have been the foundation of the extraordinary life we've built together. Thank you, Elli, for making me the luckiest man alive—I am forever grateful for you.

As I reflect on my life, I am overwhelmed with gratitude for the experiences and relationships that have shaped me. From falling out of a tree as a fearless kid to discovering my unquenchable passion for flying, my journey has been nothing short of remarkable. College, the U.S. Navy, a fulfilling career as a civilian corporate pilot, and above all, the enduring love of family—these moments have defined a life rich in adventure, meaning, and connection.

Through this book, I hope to share the stories and lessons that have brought me so much joy and fulfillment. My deepest wish is that these pages inspire you, dear reader, to explore the world with curiosity, embrace life with enthusiasm, and chase your passions and dreams with abandon. Life is an incredible adventure, waiting for you to take the controls. So buckle up, prime the throttle, engage the jet ignition, or , spin the prop, and pull the chocks. Take off into the extraordinary journey that awaits you.

And remember, before each flight—empty your bladder and fill your tanks. It's a simple rule, but trust me, it makes all the difference.

As was Jimmy's last wish, "Keep the party going"—both while we're here on this beautiful planet and later, at the ultimate going-away celebration.

With love, gratitude, and appreciation, always,

Len Curreri
Fins and Bubbles up!

CURRERI AIR

Marc's Piper Meridian "Curreri Air" taxiing out of FXE, Ft Lauderdale Executive Airport for one of the Challenge Air Flights he has supported over the years.

INTRODUCTION

As I pen these words, it has been less than a week since my former boss and dear friend, Jimmy Buffett, passed away on September 1, 2023. Whether by coincidence, serendipity, or divine intervention, that very day found me aboard my son Marc's Piper Meridian, flying from Fort Lauderdale to Scituate, Marshfield Airport (KGHG) in Massachusetts. I was serving as Marc's "Personal Radio Operator," traveling alongside his family —his wife, Jennifer, our grandsons, Jackson and Jake, and their loyal dogs, Lulu and Oliver.

During the flight, we received an unusual and unsolicited radar vectoring request from ATC Boston Center. Their instructions directed us toward Sag Harbor, New York, an area near Jimmy and Jane's home. The request was unexpected, almost uncanny, as if the universe itself had orchestrated a moment of connection.

As we passed near their beautiful residence, memories flooded back. Jimmy's home had been a special place, its dock often hosting our Amphibian Caravan for quick jaunts to the 23rd Street Seaplane Base on NYC's East River. These were adventures filled with laughter, camaraderie, and the kind of magic that only Jimmy could bring to life. This detour, entirely unplanned, gave us an extraordinary opportunity—a chance to offer an impromptu "goodbye salute" to a man who had shaped not only my career but also my life in countless meaningful ways. It was a quiet yet profound moment, filled with love and gratitude, as we flew near that familiar dock, offering our heartfelt *au revoir*.

Jimmy was more than a boss; he was an inspiration, a visionary, and a friend who touched the lives of everyone lucky enough to cross his path. He made every moment an adventure and every challenge an opportunity to find joy. His influence on me and my family was immeasurable, shaping one of the richest, most significant chapters of my journey. That flight, with its unexpected course and poignant timing, felt like a final connection—a way to honor the man who left an indelible mark on my heart and countless others.

Jimmy's spirit will live on, not only in the music and stories he shared but in the countless lives he enriched. This foreword, much like that flight, is a salute to the man who taught us all to live with a little more laughter, a lot more love, and a heart wide open to the adventures that await.

I'd like to take a moment to pay special tribute to my former "Road Wife" and invaluable Air Margaritaville team member, Captain Randall "Airial" Leslie. If you knew me—or even just knew of me—and ever went looking for me during my time with Air Margaritaville (aka Sails in Concert Inc.), chances are you spoke to Randy first. And for good reason. Randy was the heart and soul of our team and a true joy to talk to, especially when the topic turned to aviation.

Randy served as our "Official Ambassador," a title he earned through his warm personality, unmatched charisma, and extraordinary ability to connect with everyone around him. His history with Jimmy and Mrs. Buffett predated my own, beginning during his time at Business Jet at Palm Beach International Airport (PBI). It was there that he first crossed paths with Jimmy, along with Billy Schmidt, who would later become the final Air Margaritaville Flight Department Manager. From the moment I joined "Sails in Concert," it was obvious that Randy was more than a team member—he was a relationship builder in the truest sense of the word. His connections extended beyond Jimmy to Mike Ramos, the Coral Reefer Band, and the entire production crew.

Randy was an irreplaceable part of our team and a dear friend. Together, we became affectionately known as "Lenny and Squiggy"—a nickname that stuck, though to this day, I'm not entirely sure why. But it suited us. Randy brought humor, charm, and a sense of joy to every situation. His impeccable timing and quick wit could diffuse tension and brighten even the most challenging days. Whether it was resolving a tricky situation with the production crew or swapping stories with Mike Ramos, Randy had a way of making people feel valued and appreciated.

Beyond his professional contributions, Randy was a true Jimmy Buffett historian. He knew every lyric to every song, the stories behind them, and the reasons they resonated with audiences around the world. His friendships with the Coral Reefer Band and crew members were genuine and deep, always fostering a sense of camaraderie and connection wherever he went.

Today, I imagine Randy in Margaritaville Heaven, reunited with Jimmy, Ralph MacDonald, Greg "Fingers" Taylor, Larry "Groovy" Gray, Rodney Gnoinski, the "Gentle Giant" Charleston Miles, and their many mutual friends. Together, they're undoubtedly "keeping the party going—from above"— just as they did here on Earth.

Randy's life was tragically cut short on December 6, 2007, leaving a void that can never truly be filled. He is deeply missed by everyone who had the privilege of knowing and working with him. His legacy lives on in the countless lives he touched, the laughter he shared, and the friendships he built.

My favorite picture of Randy (AKA "Road Wife"

God bless Randy, Jimmy, and the entire extended Margaritaville family. Their spirit, joy, and love will forever inspire those of us who were lucky enough to be part of their world.

My time as Jimmy Buffett's flight department manager was a truly special chapter of my life. As one of the greatest entertainers of all time and the beloved leader of the "Parrot Head" community, Jimmy left an unforgettable mark on the world. In sharing my experiences, I'll offer insights and untold stories that will deepen your appreciation of his life, legacy, and spirit.

Being part of his journey was both a privilege and an honor—a true once-in-a-lifetime opportunity. My heartfelt prayers go out to Jimmy Buffett, his wife Jane, their beautiful family, and the extended Margaritaville community, including the Coral Reefer Band and the Air Margaritaville team.

INTRODUCTION • xix

The Beautiful Buffett family, Jimmy, Jane, Savannah, Delany, Cameron. This is about the time I joined "Sails in Concert, Inc." late 1999.

"JD" (JB's Dad, Delany) and JB

Throughout my years with Jimmy Buffett, I had the privilege of working alongside an incredible maintenance crew, whose dedication and camaraderie made every moment unforgettable. Even more remarkable was the opportunity to fly with Jimmy aboard the "Air Margaritaville" fleet, logging over 700 hours in the air together as we traveled the world.

Hidden Runways is a storybook of memories—both written and visual—capturing that extraordinary chapter of my life. It also weaves in stories from my years in the military, college, and adult life, including those shared by people I admire, respect, and appreciate for their impact on my journey. Many of these individuals were by my side, helping me "fact-check" my memories and ensuring the accuracy of the stories told here. From the cockpit and beyond, this book reflects the life experiences that shaped my career and the people who made it all the more meaningful.

I hope you enjoy these stories and the way they celebrate a life enriched by shared experiences with remarkable individuals. My goal is for you to find them not only interesting and entertaining but also insightful—perhaps even learning something new along the way.

The *Air Margaritaville* (also known as *Sails in Concert*) tour photos in this book come from two distinct periods of my career. The first was during my time as a charter pilot for Dave Hurley's Flight Services Group (FSG), when Jimmy chartered an 18-passenger Challenger 600 for the *Hot Water* tour from 1988 to 1989. During this time, I alternated between flying for Jimmy Buffett's tour and Jerry Garcia's *Grateful Dead* tour. A decade later, I returned to *Air Margaritaville* as Managing Director and Chief Pilot for Jimmy Buffett from 1999 to 2006.

The true value of this book lies in the depth of stories that no one else can tell—because they simply weren't there. As Managing Director and Chief Pilot for Jimmy Buffett, I had the unique responsibility of overseeing his "Air Menagerie," an eclectic fleet of land planes, seaplanes, and jets.

Since Jimmy's passing, I've read countless heartfelt messages from the "Parrot Head" community on Facebook and social media. Now, I offer my own personal recollections. To respect privacy, this book contains no private conversations—only the moments and experiences that are directly reflected in the stories and photographs shared here. Flying alongside Jimmy was an experience I will never forget. As both his Chief Pilot and Flight Instructor, I sat less than two feet away from him in the cockpit for more than 700 hours of flight time. Whether soaring in his Falcon 50, Falcon 900B, or Amphibian Caravan C-208, it was clear that his *"Son of a Son of a Sailor"* instincts extended far beyond the ocean—his airmanship and professionalism as a pilot were every bit as impressive in the sky as they were on the water.

As I began putting *pen to paper* for this book, memories of my past adventures started unfolding before me. Each moment was like a snapshot in time, a piece of a journey that, for several reasons, could never be replicated today:

1. Many of the organizations I was once affiliated with have either dissolved or merged with other like-minded companies.
2. The Federal Aviation Administration (FAA) and global private aviation regulations have evolved significantly, altering the policies, flight operations, and aviation culture that shaped my experiences.
3. The mentors and teachers who guided me along the way have either *Gone West*, passed away, are in failing health, or, in some cases, may no longer remember me.
4. The unique combination of flight, business, and social opportunities that played a role in my success simply no longer exists.
5. With the passing of my former boss, Jimmy Buffett, I will never again have the rare fortune of being in the *right place* at the *right time* to be in his employ—not just once, but twice.

For those reading this book, I can only pass along the wisdom that Jimmy Buffett lived by:

"Breathe in, breathe out, move on."

That was the paradise he created for all of us.

Someone once shared a powerful sentiment on social media—paraphrased, it went something like this:

"The earth is approximately 10 billion years old. Be thankful that we were here, at this exact moment in time, to experience and enjoy the one and only Jimmy Buffett. Appreciate it, be grateful, and relish it all."

I couldn't agree more.

As for everyone else mentioned in these vignettes, you hold a special place in my heart. Your presence, support, and influence have helped shape my career and life in ways I will always cherish.

For that, I am forever grateful.

INTRODUCTION • xxiii

Photo credits: *paulajonesphoto.com*

PREFACE

This book serves as both a travel log and a memoir of a corporate pilot who had the privilege of flying an extraordinary mix of clients over a career spanning more than 50 years. Throughout that time, I flew for companies, organizations, and individuals—each with their own unique destinations, whether for business, necessity, or simply the thrill of satisfying their curiosity.

Beyond just a collection of flight experiences, this book also offers glimpses into moments in history, each chapter reflecting a particular time and place that could never be duplicated.

Take, for example, John Hendricks—author of *A Curious Discovery: An Entrepreneur's Story* and founder of the Discovery Channel (and a close friend of Jimmy Buffett). He gave me the incredible opportunity to spend a summer as a crew member on his Falcon 900EX, flying alongside his Chief Pilot, Mike W. Those flights remain some of the most memorable and enjoyable of my career. My deepest thanks to John, Mike, Chip, and Trevor —our expert maintenance chief—for ensuring smooth sailing on every journey.

Then there was a well-known confectionery company— perhaps you've heard of Mentos? Their fleet of aircraft ranged from jets to turboprops to general aviation planes, and for over two decades, I had the pleasure of flying with their outstanding team, primarily out of Lugano, Switzerland, as well as other fascinating locations around the world. As their *Alien Training Provider*, I remained closely connected to the company, and those years provided some of my greatest flying memories.

To Giorgio P., Edigio P., Carlo S., Willy H., Andrea M., Brenno B., Alois L., and Luca S.—*Mille Grazie!* Your professionalism, camaraderie, and passion for aviation made every flight an unforgettable adventure.

Falcon 100 and Falcon 900EX—were the aircraft I spent the most time flying with the confectionery group. These birds carried us on countless journeys, each flight adding to a lifetime of unforgettable experiences. Though they have since retired to serve new owners, their legacy in my career remains indelible.

Then there were Kris S., Heinz K., and Armado of Fairwind Inc., Jet Aviation—people who provided me with the incredible opportunity to fly to new destinations, including Panama and beyond, alongside Captains Mike A. and Ray H. I also had the privilege of pairing up with my longtime friend, John Kermashek, and our trusted professional flight attendant, Hazel Hesp. Hazel, known for her resilience as a flight attendant on the hijacked TWA Flight #847 from Athens to Rome (with its final destination in Beirut, Lebanon), was part of some of the most intriguing and unforgettable adventures of my career. Even now, many of those experiences still seem unbelievable.

Every one of these individuals was an exceptional pilot, crew member, and teacher, and together, we shared adventures that were not only remarkable but, in some cases, downright challenging and disruptive. I consider it a privilege to pass along these stories.

After my tenure with Jimmy Buffett, I established *L&E Consultants, Inc.* in Florida, with just two employees—my wife,

Elena(Elli), and myself. My focus was aviation-related, while Elli's expertise was in real estate. We incorporated in the State of Florida, and to this day, we remain an active business.

For years, I had considered writing my memoir. But it was Jimmy's passing that became my *tipping point*—a stark reminder of my own mortality and the realization that if I was serious about documenting my life's journey, I needed to start while my memory was still sharp. In my last direct communication with Jimmy this past spring, he told me that he liked to keep in touch with all his "AOs." If you're wondering what an "AO" is, it stands for *Active Octogenarian*—a club I'm proud to have belonged to alongside him.

This book is more than just a collection of my stories—it's also a tribute to Jimmy Buffett and the impact he had on my life.

Each chapter, or *Flight*, will chronicle different decades of my journey, beginning in the 1950s in my hometown of Quincy, Massachusetts. From there, these *Flights* will take you through the many places my career has brought me—across the globe, to nearly every corner of the planet, except for two countries I have yet to visit... *Australia and New Zealand*.

My Family: Marc, Cristina, Me and Elli at a Jimmy Buffett show in Great Woods Venue

My family visit with Jimmy Buffett before a Great Woods Show

FLIGHT 01L

My First "Wheels"

I grew up in Quincy (pronounced *Quinzy*), Massachusetts—the *City of Presidents*, home to both John Adams, the second U.S. President, and his son, John Quincy Adams, the sixth. In fact, I lived less than a thousand feet from their actual birthplace in South Quincy, at 19 Trescott Street.

But what truly shaped my childhood wasn't just the rich history surrounding me—it was the proximity to *Quincy Gas*, also known as *Adams Service Station*. This wasn't just any gas station;

it was owned by Joe Iacobucci, a World War II B-17 mechanic and fellow Quiet Birdman (QB), who had a deep passion for aviation.

Joe wasn't just a mechanic—he was a caretaker of history, owning and maintaining several vintage airplanes. Some of these aircraft were housed right at his gas station, just a five-minute walk from my house. To the astonishment of passersby, Joe would chain down the tail of his *Aeronca Champ 7AC* and *Fairchild F-24* and perform full engine run-ups right there on the lot. The sight—and sound—of those engines roaring to life in the middle of a neighborhood gas station was nothing short of mesmerizing.

Joe's Antique Fairchild 24, powered by a Warner Scarab rotary engine - another Iacobucci masterpiece from his gas station hangar to her new nest at Plymouth Airport hangar.

Joe Iacobucci planted the seeds of my lifelong love affair with aviation. More than just a mentor, he introduced me to *U-control* model airplanes, sparking my fascination with flight at an early age. Joe knew I couldn't afford my own airplane—despite juggling three paper routes (*Quincy Patriot Ledger, Boston Globe,* and *Boston Herald*) and working as a clerk at the *Great Atlantic & Pacific Tea Company* market. But that didn't matter to him.

Instead, he instilled in me a deep passion for aviation and opened the door to a world I never could have accessed on my own.

It was Joe who introduced me to the *Civil Air Patrol (CAP)*—the official auxiliary of the U.S. Air Force—during my teenage years in the 1950s. I was hooked.

To earn every possible ride in Joe's aircraft, I worked hard—anything to get a seat in the cockpit. His planes were kept at a makeshift airfield in Braintree, a place known back then as a *"self-defense" airport*. Located near the Great Pond Dam, the strip constantly required maintenance and tree trimming to keep the runway clear for takeoff and landing. Keeping it operational was an uphill battle, but to me, it was a gateway to the skies.

I was so *gung ho* about CAP that I spent my hard-earned money on the best uniforms I could buy. I wanted my fellow cadets to know that I was serious about aviation. And I was. Every flight, every lesson, and every experience fueled my determination to make flying my life's work.

I eventually earned the rank of *Cadet Commander* of the NAS South Weymouth Squadron, which was based at the old NAS South Weymouth blimp hangar. That massive structure served as the site for our drills and meetings, and every time I stepped inside, I couldn't help but imagine the enormous U.S. Navy dirigibles—*Submarine Hunters*—that had once been housed there. It amazed me to think about these massive airships patrolling the skies at such slow speeds, playing a vital role in maritime defense.

It was during this time that I experienced my very first airplane ride in a *Civil Air Patrol L-16A*—a military variant of the *Aeronca Champ 7AC*, outfitted with an extra five-gallon auxiliary fuel tank. The flight took off from Norwood Airport, with *CAP Senior Lt. Walter Hanson* at the controls. He made sure that my first real flight was one I would never forget. From that moment on, there was no turning back—aviation had its grip on me for life.

I'll never forget the moment I watched the earth's surface drift farther and farther away from the aircraft, mesmerized by the sensation of leaving the ground behind. Little did I know that 35 years later, in 1991, I would find myself looking out the small cabin windows of the *Concorde*, soaring at *60,000 feet*—so high that I could actually see the curvature of the earth. But more on that later.

However, my entire aviation journey could have been *preempted* if things had turned out differently on one particular afternoon at *Adams Elementary School*.

It was the end of a school day, and as I stepped outside, I noticed an elderly woman standing near the entrance. She was stopping young boys, asking them a question. Curious, and eager to help—after all, I *was* a Boy Scout—I approached her.

She explained that she needed a favor. There was a *pignut tree* near the front door of the school, and she wanted someone to climb it and shake the branches so she could collect the fallen nuts to bake a pie. In exchange, she offered me *25 cents*.

I agreed. Without hesitation, I climbed the tree, making my way about halfway up before shaking the branches. As expected, *pignuts rained down*. Mission accomplished.

But as I prepared to descend, my grip suddenly slipped.

I fell.

Bouncing off several branches on the way down, I crashed onto the hard tarmac—landing with my full body weight on my right hand. When I looked at it, I was horrified. My hand had *bent completely backward*, the palm nearly covering my wrist like a pancake. Pain shot through me, but somehow, I was alive.

The old woman? *Gone without a trace.*

Now I had to figure out how to get home and find a doctor *ASAP*.

The walk back to *19 Trescott Street* usually took ten minutes, but I decided to take a shortcut through a neighbor's property. Unfortunately, they had installed a *brand-new fence* just the day before, blocking my path. I had no choice but to take the long way home—doubling my journey while cradling my injured hand.

When I finally arrived, my mother was home, but my father was on duty at *Engine 3 Fire Station*, too far away to leave work and help me.

Desperate, I made a call to *Joe Iacobucci*—the same Joe who had introduced me to aviation. In addition to his love for airplanes, Joe owned *Quincy Cab*, and without hesitation, he arranged transportation to *Quincy City Hospital*.

Thank *God* for Joe.

The on-duty doctor in the emergency room took one look at my wrist—bent completely out of its natural position—and instructed me to look away. Before I could process what was happening, he *twisted* my wrist back into place. A sharp jolt of pain shot through me, but almost instantly, I felt a wave of relief. Afterward, they set my wrist in a cast, and just like that, I had survived what I now consider a major *Change of Life (COL)* moment.

Looking back, I realized I had made a *stupid* mistake—not fully considering the potential consequences of my eager attempt to be a *good Boy Scout* and, perhaps, earn another merit badge in the process. Lesson learned.

The 1950s were a time when I poured every bit of personal time into anything that could *enhance* my aviation education. If I had extra cash from one of my jobs, I spent it building model airplanes in the cellar of *Bill Ellis's* home on Federal Avenue. It was my way of staying connected to aviation, even when I wasn't in the cockpit.

By 1959, I graduated from *Quincy High School* with an *A+* in *Mr. Grassie's* aeronautics class—a small but proud accomplishment that reinforced my passion for flight. From there, I applied to *Boston University* and was thrilled to be accepted.

But there was one problem: tuition.

At *$513 per semester*, it was *barely* within reach. Determined to make it work, I picked up another job—this time, making *false teeth* alongside one of my closest friends, *Jimmy Mezzetti*. Jimmy and I bonded over our shared love of aviation and model-building, but there was something else that made him stand out—his *1957 Chevy with Turnpike Skirts*.

Back then, that car was the definition of *hot*.

2
FLIGHT 02R
Circa 1950–1960s

D'Andrea photo among well over a million distinctly
different guitar picks produced for customers

After two demanding years at *Boston University*, I was ready for a change—new surroundings, new friends, and, most importantly, a fresh academic environment. I had spent those years as a *BU day-hop*, commuting from home and saving as much money as possible for tuition, room, and board. That financial discipline allowed me to transfer to *Parks College of Aeronautics* at *Saint Louis University*—the oldest government-certified aviation school in the country and one of the most highly respected.

Parks College did not disappoint. The experience, education, and aviation-focused environment profoundly shaped my future in ways I never could have imagined.

One unexpected surprise was meeting *Tony D'Andrea*, whose father owned *D'Andrea Manufacturing*—the company responsible for producing guitar picks for some of the biggest names in the music industry, including *Jimmy Buffett's Coral Reefer Band*.

It's funny how life works—who would have thought that attending an aviation school would eventually connect me to *JB... through guitar picks?*

Jimmy Buffett pick, circa mid-1990's.

Although I didn't receive formal flight training at *Parks College*, I still found opportunities to fly—though in a rather unconventional way. As part of the school's flying club, the *Cessna 140 "Sky Snoopers"*, I embarked on an unforgettable journey from *Cahokia, Illinois* to *West Palm Beach, Florida* alongside my roommate and pilot extraordinaire, *Art Danley*.

We flew *IFR*—not the standard *Instrument Flight Rules*, but rather *"I Fly Railroads"*. Since most of the navigation equipment onboard didn't work (including the *Mitchell Boy* navigation radio), we literally followed the railway tracks all the way to West Palm Beach, using little more than our eyes, ears, and instincts.

Art was nothing short of exceptional—he went on to become one of the youngest *TWA pilots* at just 21 years old and later made history as the youngest Boeing 707 captain. I owe Art a great deal for helping me grasp the fundamentals of flight and, just as importantly, teaching me how to properly communicate with *Air Traffic Control (ATC)*—a skill that would serve me well throughout my career.

During my first year at *Parks College*, I made a major decision—one that I didn't share with my parents at the time. In 1961, I enlisted in the *U.S. Navy* at *NAS Olathe, Kansas*, anticipating that it would give me a head start in seniority within the officer ranks and provide financial assistance to help pay off my college loans after completing *Aviation Officer Candidate School (AOCs)*. It turned out to be one of the best decisions I ever made, allowing me to pay off my loans much faster than I had anticipated.

The two years I spent at *Parks College* were filled with new experiences and lifelong friendships. Joining the *Phi Alpha Chi* social and professional aviation fraternity and earning *CHI officer status* exposed me to a wealth of aviation knowledge and camaraderie. I also got my fair share of Jesuit education, taking philosophical and religious courses taught by priests who had larger-than-life personalities—some of whom were pilots themselves.

One of the more unique characters was *Father Higgins*, known for his ability to hypnotize students dealing with psychological or physiological issues. I sought out his help when I struggled to stomach the food at the school cafeteria, known for its infamous meals served by *Ma Hahn* and the *Spoon Lady*. Father "Higgy" did his best to hypnotize me into tolerating the food, and while his method worked *for a short time*, it never fully cured my distaste for cafeteria-prepared meals.

1962 Pledge Class in front of the famous and well-visited "Ranch"

Father Chopesky (affectionately known as *"The Chopper"*), who was the Dean of *Parks College* during my first year, was well-liked and always entertaining to watch as he flew the school's airplanes in the campus runway pattern. Then there was a priest who patrolled the hallways like a sentry, on the lookout for students engaging in activities that didn't align with Jesuit expectations. Some got caught, others managed to slip away. For those who weren't so lucky, the price of *forgiveness* came in the form of penance, prayer, and unwanted work assignments that cut into our social schedules. But somehow, we all survive

Becoming a *Phi Alpha Chi* fraternity brother was one of the highlights of my time at *Parks College*. It was an extraordinary group—each member with a unique personality and skill set—

reinforcing that my decision to attend *Parks* had been the right one.

One brother, *Ray Valeika*, stood out among us all. His story was nothing short of remarkable. He and his family had *escaped* Communist-occupied Lithuania and sought refuge in the U.S. His journey was already inspiring, but what truly set him apart was his unwavering resilience. While he was still a student at *Parks College*, both of his parents tragically passed away, leaving him to support his siblings on his own. Despite these hardships, Ray exceeded all expectations, building an exceptional airline career that led him to senior-level maintenance positions at *Pan Am, Continental, and Delta Airlines*.

His story was just one of many that made *Parks College* such a special place—a melting pot of talent, determination, and brotherhood.

I unexpectedly earned my *FAA Powerplant Mechanic's* license while attending *Parks College*. One day, I received a call from an FAA-designated examiner specializing in helicopter maintenance, who had tracked me down as a candidate for the Powerplant Mechanics category. He offered me an opportunity to take the test, and despite having no tools, I still had a wealth of knowledge stored in my brain from *BU's Aeronautical Technology* course. So, I decided to take him up on his offer—and it turned out to be a lot of fun.

The test began with the *Continental A65* engine in the test cell. I was tasked with checking the engine timing. Following the instructions in the maintenance manual, I worked through the procedure. After a few hiccups, the engine ran normally, and I passed an important part of the practical exam.

Next, I was asked to explain the function of a *Hamilton Standard Reversible Prop*. Once again, I managed to provide a satisfactory response.

Finally, I was challenged to start the A65 without a starter. Summoning my courage, I stepped up, flipped the prop by hand, and successfully started the engine—without losing any fingers.

That skill came in handy 35 years later in *Germany*, when I had to hand-prop *Bernhard Conrad's Aeronca Chief*—a story you'll read about later in this book.

It was a momentous day when the FAA examiner signed off on my *FAA A&P Mechanic's* license. In fact, I earned it before the U.S. even had ZIP codes, which were established the following year, on July 1, 1963.

On the afternoon of *August 4th*, while serving as *SDO (Squadron Duty Officer)*, I received an urgent communication from *CINC-PACFLT* reporting that the destroyers *Maddox* and *Turner Joy* had allegedly been attacked by *North Vietnamese torpedo boats*. At the time, our ship was anchored in *Hong Kong Harbor*, and every man was ordered to return immediately.

To reach the skipper, I had to take a *Walla Walla (water taxi)* to *BD's shore social quarters* at the *Park Hotel, Suite 1501*. I personally handed him the communique, which would later be documented in the *CIA's "Command History of the USS Constellation, CVA-64."*

Captain *Fred A. Bardshar*, our CO, wasted no time. Over the ship's *bullhorn*,

he gave the command:
"Man your battle stations!"

With that, we raised anchor and moved into international waters. Four hours later, just after midnight, our Scooters launched—engaging the *alleged* North Vietnamese torpedo boats.

And as they say, "the rest is history."

It would be another two years before I finally began civilian flight training. At 24 years old, I started my flying lessons and was eventually cleared for solo by *Bert Steele*. On May 17, 1965, I completed my first solo flight at *Auxiliary Field #5* near *MCAS Yuma, AZ*, during a Navy weapons deployment.

Shortly thereafter, I joined one of the Navy's famed *"Bird Farms"*, the *USS Ranger (CVA-61)*, and headed west to join the *Gulf of Tonkin Yacht Club*—stationed at *Point Yankee* with *Air Group 14*.

HOTO VA-146 "The World Famous Blue Diamonds" – Circa 1965–1966. Photo credit: U.S. Navy

3

FLIGHT 03L

Circa 1960–1970s

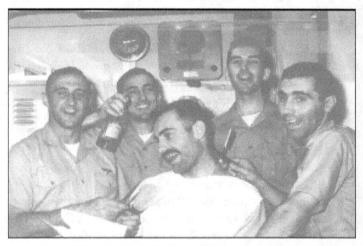

A special VA-146 haircut for the "hairiest" shipmate, Jim "RAH" Childs, in the middle with a white drape, from LCDR Neil Gerl, LT Bert Steele, LTJG Neville Haggerty, and me, Ensign Len Curreri

After a brief respite on the ground at *NAS Lemoore*, the *Blue Diamond* personnel—excluding the pilots, who would fly out to the *USS Ranger (CVA-61)* later—packed up and embarked on the carrier. With *VA-146 Blue Diamonds'* 14 Douglas A-4C "Scooters", our pilots were preparing for combat sorties and would soon face the realities of war alongside our comrades in arms.

After successfully completing our Operational Readiness Inspection (ORI) during our second combat cruise with *Carrier Air Wing 14*, I found myself in an unexpected position—I was now *officially* the only civilian Private Pilot among the *VA-146 "World Famous Blue Diamonds"* Navy Aviators. To mark the occasion, our skipper, CDR Hugh B. Loheed, a fellow Massachusetts native, personally presented me with my own wings in *Hawaii*. It was an incredible honor.

Unfortunately, this deployment also brought devastating losses.

Our beloved skipper, CDR Hugh B. Loheed (from *Middleboro, MA*), was Killed in Action (KIA) after being shot down by anti-aircraft artillery (AAA) over North Vietnam on *February 1, 1966*. Below is his obituary:

"Captain Loheed was the commanding officer of Attack Squadron 146, Carrier Air Wing 14 aboard the Aircraft Carrier USS RANGER (CVA-61). On February 1, 1966, he was the pilot of a Douglas Attack Aircraft Skyhawk (A-4C) attacking targets in Nghe An Province, North Vietnam, five miles northeast of Phu Dien Chau, when contact was lost. His remains were recovered on August 16, 1986, and identified on August 15, 1994."

His wingman, Ensign Jeff "Leprechaun" Greenwood, survived the mission and returned safely to the *Ranger*.

Another fellow pilot, Hugh "Slugger" Magee, was shot down by *AAA* over *North Vietnam* in *"Busy Bee" 604, A-4C BN 149571*. He ejected and was successfully recovered on *May 25, 1966*.

One of my most influential mentors during this time was Bert Steele, a significant figure in my aviation journey. Bert was the instructor who *soloed me* at *Auxiliary Field #5 in Yuma, Arizona*, just a few miles north of the Mexican border. My first solo flight, in a Cessna 150 (N6240T), was witnessed by *Bert* and a gathering of curious *prairie dogs*.

Bert also allowed me the privilege of flying his privately owned Taylorcraft BC-12D (N44496), a beautifully maintained aircraft that he kept in a barn on a local farmer's property near

NAS Lemoore, California. It was an unforgettable experience, and Bert's guidance played a major role in shaping the aviator I would become.

Flying this magnificent machine in 1965 came at an out-of-pocket cost of just $1.35 per hour for 80-octane aviation gasoline, plus $0.35 for oil. That was what we called an "all wet" deal. The only catch? If we crashed it, we bought it—because it wasn't insured.

Poor Neville Haggerty, who had the same arrangement for flying this aircraft, learned that lesson the hard way. One day, he applied just a little too much pressure on the heel brakes during landing. The plane flipped tail over nose, leaving him and his only passenger—his soon-to-be wife—hanging upside down by their seatbelts. Fortunately, there was no fire, no flames, and aside from their bruised egos, they were completely unharmed.

The total replacement cost of the aircraft? Approximately $700. That's it.

Upon returning from VA-146, Air Group 14, and CVA-64's first and longest combat cruise, the USS Constellation's Flag Officer was tasked with producing a Combat Pennant (officially called a "Homeward-Bound" Pennant). The requirement? It had to be equal to the ship's length—1,048 feet—but could not exceed the total number of personnel aboard, which was approximately 5,00

Rough seas during "Underway replenishment)) Photo credit - Len Currreri

4
FLIGHT 04R

On my 1966 USS Ranger second combat cruise, our skipper, call sign "S-14" (for the number of letters in his last name and his shoe size), Albert Schaufelberger, the Commanding Officer of VA-146, led a *gaggle* of 22 aircraft from Air Wing Group 14 to strike a primary target during Operation Rolling Thunder. Their objective was the oil and petroleum (POL) deposits in Haiphong, North Vietnam—one of the most heavily defended targets, protected by AAA (anti-aircraft artillery) and SAMs (surface-to-air missiles).

I vividly remember standing on the USS Ranger's flight deck, counting each aircraft as they returned. The moment felt eerily reminiscent of watching *Victory at Sea* documentaries on black-and-white television as a kid—except this was real.

One by one, I counted the returning aircraft:
- RA-5C Vigilantes from RVAH-5, most critical on fuel.
- F-4B squadrons VF-142 and VF-143 ("Puking Dogs").
- A-4C and A-4Es from VA-146 and VA-55.
- VAW-11 E-2A for early warning.
- A-3D Skywarriors from VAH-10, serving as tankers.
- Lastly, the A-1H Skyraiders (Spads) from VA-145, whose pilots carried their trusty *rubber doughnuts*—hemorrhoid cushions for those long flights.

To my relief, *every aircraft that launched for the Haiphong POL mission returned.* Some bore minor bullet holes, but all were safe, secure, and flyable enough to make it back to the ship. That day, every single pilot made it home.

Unfortunately, the overall combat cruise was costly. In addition to the 15 combat losses, we suffered six operational losses:

- January 16, 1966 – Loss of an RA-5C Vigilante from RVAH-9, both crew members killed.

- January 25, 1966 – Loss of an A-4E Skyhawk from VA-55, pilot recovered.

- June 1, 1966 – Loss of another A-4E from VA-55, pilot recovered.

- June 20, 1966 – Loss of an A-1H Skyraider from VA-145, pilot killed.

- July 11, 1966 – Loss of an F-4B Phantom II from VF-143, both crew members recovered.

During my final weeks on active duty with VA-146 at NAS Lemoore, California, I had the rare privilege of actually flying with a fellow *Blue Diamond* "Scooter" pilot, Ensign Evan Totten. While it wasn't in an A-4C Skyhawk, we flew together—Evan in a Piper Cherokee and me in a Cessna 180. We communicated just as we would in a combat formation, using our call signs "BusyBee 1" and "BusyBee 2" over VHF. Though it was a civilian flight, it was an unforgettable way to close my active-duty career with the *World Famous Blue Diamonds*.

After mustering out of VA-146 on January 17, 1967, I never lost touch with my squadron mates. For over 57 years, we have remained connected. The Blue Diamonds are more than just a squadron—they are family, and I will carry that bond with me for the rest of my life.

Two active VFA-146 pilots visiting the Hemisphere Dancer.
Picture credit — Chris Dixon

Admiral Mike Bowman and JB piloting the Hemisphere Dancer.

Before I leave this previously hidden runway, I have a light-hearted story I thought would be safe to share, since it was all in the spirit of helping out a shipmate.

My bunkmate, our Landing Signal Officer (LSO), was recovering from a common ailment among Attack/Fighter pilots—those who "pull" a lot of Gs during high-stress sorties.

His wife, Sue, along with "Goose" G's wife, Nancy, were what we jokingly referred to as *camp followers*—faithfully traveling from port to port to spend as much time as possible with their husbands.

One night, Sue asked if she could use my bunk so she could stay overnight and help nurse Bill back to good health. Since our ship was tied up at the Subic Bay dock, I didn't think it would be an issue. I had squadron mates with an extra empty bunk in their stateroom, so I had a place to crash for the night.

The next morning, Sue stepped out onto the starboard catwalk—similar to the area where our Blue Diamond "Scooters" were parked on the flight deck—to dry her red hair in the open air. That's when the ship's captain, McCuddin, decided to use the ship's bullhorn—broadcast across the entire vessel—and announced:

"Will the sailor in the red dress (actually her bathrobe) please report to the bridge"

" I can't remember if he actually said "please," but the message was clear.

This was the same skipper who once ordered the *purple shirts* (refueling crew) to throw used jet oil cans overboard so he could practice skeet shooting from the bridge between aircraft launches!

Sue, now mortified, reported to the bridge, escorted by our CO, Skipper "S-14," to meet the ship's captain. Though McCuddin was known for having a sense of humor—he even dressed up a female mannequin named "Kuddles" and placed her in the captain's chair for morale purposes—this was *not* one of those moments.

For more on that story, see the article below from the CVA-61 USS Ranger Cruise Book.

Special thanks to VA-146 AE Al Herman, who joined the squadron on the same day as me—June 22, 1964

Area where sailor in the red dress was spotted.

Entering the Blue Diamond alley

I entered the *Blue Diamond* Alley and Ready Room on CVA-64, USS Constellation, to start my day as the squadron Duty Officer.

Blue Diamond Ordnance team (Red Shirts) manually loading a MK 84, 2000 lb low-drag bomb—each man sharing 167 lbs of the load by crossing hands. That's me, top second from the left.

Needless to say, I soon found myself in a private audience with our CO, S-14. By the end of the conversation, he softened, adopting a humorous—but firm—tone as he gave me strict orders: "Don't do that again." In retrospect, I would have been better served and would have been wiser to contact Skipper S-24 first!

More than anything, I was concerned about how this might impact S-14's own Fitness Report and his path toward becoming an admiral. But he reassured me that the *Red Dress* incident had no negative effect on his evaluation—or mine—and that I had nothing to worry about.

In the end, the skipper's Fitness Report focused on what really mattered—his leadership in managing 22 aircraft combat sorties, a feat that was considered a major success by anyone's analysis. He always said, *"We all rise on someone else's shoulders and put the troops first."* That mindset defined his leadership.

S-14 wasn't just a great and inspiring career naval officer; he was a special human being. I will be forever grateful to have served under his command.

As for Bill, he was more than happy to have his wife there to help him recover from a *very common* medical issue among carrier pilots. A lot of other guys onboard the Ranger suffered from the same problem but didn't have their wives around to help them along—especially the Spad drivers, who were usually the first to launch and the last to recover from any mission.

Years later, after Bill left the Navy and became a TWA pilot, he was diagnosed with a malignant brain tumor about two years into his employment. By 1992, he was wheelchair-bound, and during a Falcon 50 trip near his home in Saint Louis, Missouri, I had the chance to visit him along with his new wife, Nancy.

Nancy told me that Bill didn't have much time left and that he had been severely depressed—he rarely smiled anymore. Wanting to lift his spirits, I leaned in and whispered in his ear, reminding him of the infamous *Sailor in the Red Dress Incident*.

For the first time in a long while, Bill *perked up and broke into a big smile*.

That moment made our day—and his.

Humor, no matter what condition you're in, almost always serves as a powerful remedy.

A Fort Myers, Florida mini-reunion with VA-146 World Famous Blue Diamond squadron mates—Bert Steele, Bill Douglas, Neal Gerl, and me.

5
FLIGHT 05L

After one of our port visits to Yokosuka, Japan, we were cruising on the USS Ranger along the Japanese east coast, heading toward our station at Point Yankee in the Gulf of Tonkin, when we were informed that we would be receiving a special visit from a USO tour.

The lineup included Bob Hope, Louis "Satchmo" Armstrong, Johnny Unitas (the legendary Baltimore Colts quarterback), and a very special guest—Ann-Margret.

One of our sister squadron *"Garfish"* VA-55 pilots, LT Rich Allen, had a unique connection to Ann-Margret. As it turned out, they had been former classmates—and more—at Northwestern University in Chicago. When Rich casually mentioned this, a few of our fellow Naval Aviators, ever skeptical, dismissed it as just another *aviation tall tale*. Naturally, bets were placed.

Ann-Margret entering the VA-55 Garfish *Ready Room*

As fate would have it, when Ann-Margret stepped through the Ready Room door—with the Ranger's XO directly behind her—she immediately blurted out in excitement,

"Rich, what are you doing here?"

Without missing a beat, Rich grinned and replied, "What d'ya think? I'm in the Navy!"

The room erupted in cheers and laughter, and the VA-55 Skipper couldn't help but play along.

"Okay, you're relieved of OPS for the day! Go ahead and take her around the ship."

Ann-Margret's initial reaction to seeing Rich!

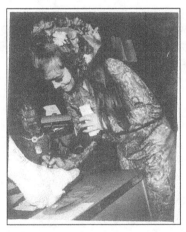

Ann-Margret signing Rich's foot cast—which was not a combat wound, but an injury from falling off a barstool at the Subic Bay 'O' Club!

After showing Ann-Margret around the ship, Rich escorted her to a helicopter for her return to Japan—much to the disappointment of the Ranger's ship's company, Air Group 14 pilots, and staff. I would have loved to be a *fly on the wall* to hear the chatter afterward!

This wasn't just another case of Aviator's embellishment—it was a true story.

LT Rich Allen later went on to earn a Distinguished Flying Cross (DFC) and had a distinguished Navy career, including serving as Commanding Officer of Naval Reserve CV-63 Unit.

6
FLIGHT 06R

Upon leaving NAS Lemoore on January 16, 1967, I jumped into my brand-new 1967 MGB-GT (see above), still sporting its United Kingdom number plate, JGT663D—which, to my good fortune, I was able to keep for almost two years. My destination was Burnside-Ott Aviation School in Opa-Locka, Florida, where I would begin basic training for my FAA Commercial and Instrument ratings.

No fancy airplanes—just a Cessna 150 and Cessna 172.

To make ends meet, I worked nights as an A&P mechanic,

performing daily and monthly inspections in exchange for bartered flight time and extra money to offset my training costs. The GI Bill hadn't kicked in yet—it wouldn't start until September 1967—so I had to find creative ways to fund my civilian pilot's licenses.

By working and flying nonstop, I managed to earn my FAA Commercial license on March 1, 1967, and my Instrument rating on March 22, 1967—just over a month after arriving in Opa-Locka.

With those two key licenses in hand, I decided it was time to find my first real aviation job.

As luck would have it, I landed a position with Butler Aviation, a Fixed Base Operation (FBO) Chain, at their LaGuardia Airport (LGA) facility. I worked the graveyard shift as an operations supervisor—a non-flying gig, but one that placed me at the heart of corporate aviation.

The Butler facility at LGA housed an impressive collection of corporate and private aircraft, including:

- ITT Inc. with four Gulfstream G-1s and a Boeing 727
- International Paper with a Falcon 20 and Gulfstream G-1
- A Convair 240, once owned by Joe Kennedy
- A Douglas B-23, owned by Juan Trippe, the legendary CEO of Pan Am
- A Beech D50C Twin Bonanza
- A Twin Beech, owned by Doubleday Publications

The Douglas B-23, despite never seeing combat, had a unique legacy and was captained by Jack Doswell—who, within the next two years, would become my first boss.

But my time at Butler Aviation wasn't just about airplanes—it also introduced me to Frank Sinatra and his young wife, Mia Farrow.

One night, around midnight, Sinatra arrived in his Hawker 400, which he had named "Christina" after his mother. After exchanging quick hellos, he settled in with a few more drinks—

adding to the many he had likely enjoyed on the flight from Los Angeles to LaGuardia.

And then, out of nowhere, he started yelling profanities at me.

Drink in hand, he let loose—a drunken tirade that I was both stunned by and amused to witness firsthand.

Moments later, he stumbled out of his Hawker 400 and collapsed into his waiting limo—almost leaving Mia behind.

Needless to say, she was not pleased.

Standing alone on the tarmac, she seemed more *miffed* than *shocked*—as if Sinatra's dramatic exit was just another chapter in a very eventful marriage.

7
FLIGHT 07L

As the night supervisor for Butler Aviation-LGA, I used my daylight hours to scout around for flying gigs to build my flight hours. I managed to fly as a FAR 135 co-pilot for Captain Butch B. on a Beech D50C Twin Bonanza that belonged to *VIP Air*. I also got to fly Doubleday's Twin Beech and, most excitingly, had my first Falcon corporate jet ride —a trip to Montreal as a guest of International Paper's Chief Pilot, Art Blomgren.

This was an exciting time in the rapid expansion of Corporate (Business) Aviation. Around that time, a sharp lawyer named Matt Weisman launched a new business aviation management company with the help of Bill Watt and Joe Carfagana, both veterans in the field. To generate business, Matt placed an ad in Forbes magazine, promoting his company's services.

He started with a Piper Apache, then moved on to a Piper Aztec, and by the time I arrived, he was flying an Aero Commander 500. His Chief Pilot, Sy Olanoff, was a highly skilled aviator. I shared my enthusiasm for flying with Sy, hoping to join his new company, Executive Air Fleet Inc. (EAF). Around this time, EAF acquired a Beech Queen Air Model 65, a former IBM fleet aircraft from Paris, France. This plane had something I had never seen before—a Bendix Flight Director—and I was eager to get my hands on it.

Matt and Sy offered me a chance to join EAF as a crew member, but there was one big condition: I had to earn my Multi-Engine Land (MEL) rating within a few weeks before their first client trip. The opportunity was too good to pass up. The captain I'd be paired with also had a passion for music—something I could appreciate, even if I was a lousy saxophone player.

Now, I just had to find a way to earn my MEL rating—fast.

I started asking around and learned about an FAA Designated Pilot Examiner (DPE) based at Teterboro, New Jersey (TEB) who had a Grumman G-44 amphibian and the availability to train me.

I just needed to find the money.

The DPE's name was George Lambros, and his price was $350 for the MEL rating. I asked my dad if he could loan me the funds, and thankfully, he agreed.

Training in the G-44, N1340V, was an absolute blast. It had Ranger engines, wooden fixed-pitch propellers, and wooden carburetor knobs, making it one of the most unique aircraft I had flown at that point in my young aviation career. We flew around the Tappan Zee Bridge, then practiced touch-and-goes at North Haven Airport on Long Island.

It was pure fun—especially since I already had quite a bit of taildragger experience, which helped me handle the Widgeon with ease.

On our way back to TEB, George suddenly asked, "Want to try a water landing in the Hackensack River?"

I didn't hesitate—"Yes!"

That flight turned out to be a teaser that would have a major impact on my aviation career in the years to come.

After three splashes and dashes, we landed and began the debrief. George then hit me with an unexpected offer:

"For another $150, I'll add a Multi-Engine Sea (MES) rating to your license."

I was ecstatic but didn't want to push my luck by asking my *banker* (aka my dad) for another loan. In hindsight, I should have.

Earning my MEL in the G-44 on May 29, 1967, was enough to meet the entry requirements for the EAF co-pilot position, which would be a two-month assignment and give me valuable international experience in Mexico and Central America.

I quit my job at Butler Aviation and began training for my new role at EAF.

By that time, I had about 500 flight hours, and my captain allowed me to sit in the left seat during deadhead legs. After 20 hours, we alternated seats, which helped me build valuable Multi-Engine Land (MEL) time, some Pilot-in-Command (PIC) time, and international experience—all key additions to my aviation resume.

Enter the G.I. Bill. There was no way I was going to waste or pass up a free education, so I headed back to Florida and enrolled in the Certified Flight Instructor (CFI) program at Burnside-Ott in Opa-Locka.

On December 28, 1967, I earned my CFI-Instrument (CFI-I). I chose the instrument rating instructor first because I had extensive experience using IFR procedures, having flown out of one of the busiest airports in the country, LaGuardia (LGA).

On January 29, 1968, I earned my CFI-Airplane (CFI-A)—all without having to take on any additional educational loans.

With those credentials in hand, I started searching for a FAA CFI job to continue building my flight hours.

Then, out of the blue, I received a call from a company in Long Beach, California (LGB) asking if I was interested in teaching in Beechcraft Musketeers.

I really didn't have much of a choice—my cash burn was starting to impact my social life, and my new MGB-GT was proving to be more high-maintenance than I had anticipated!

After about a month in Long Beach, I got a surprise call from my mother. Someone from Gillette Company Flight Operations had contacted her, looking for me to be a fill-in co-pilot and mechanic until their usual co-pilot could get his medical certificate reinstated.

I immediately called Gillette, and they asked, "How soon can you get back to Boston?"

My answer?

"I'll be on the next airliner heading east!"

I left my MGB-GT behind to be picked up by my future brother-in-law, Ciro D'Angelo, and boarded the next flight back home.

This opportunity was too good to pass up. As part of my contract, Gillette would send me to a FlightSafety Gulfstream 1 class, covering all expenses, including room and board, while I was in training.

I couldn't believe my good fortune—it was definitely worth resigning from instructing in *"Mouseketeers"*!

However, before I could officially start, Gillette's Medical Department required me to pass a full medical examination—far beyond any standard FAA AME Class exam.

This included a heart stress test and an exhaustive battery of medical screenings—every test imaginable.

It was clear that flying for Gillette meant operating at the highest professional standards, and I was eager to prove myself up to the task.

Gillette Gulfstream 1 (G-159) N15GP in Van Dusen Hangar, BOS (Circa 1968)

I began my Indoc training at Boston Logan Airport (BOS), where Gillette's Gulfstream 1 was based at a local FBO—not far from where I had attended Boston University for my FAA Airframe and Powerplant (A&P) classes over eight years earlier (formerly the New England Aircraft School).

My Gillette instructor, Franny MacIntire, was a highly experienced former U.S. Navy PBY mechanic who filled my brain with enough information to satisfy FAA FAR Part 61.55, ensuring I was legally qualified to serve as a crew member on a Transport Category aircraft (over 12,500 pounds).

The very next day, I was on my first trip—BOS to FLL, nonstop.

Gillette's Chief Pilot, Horace Wood, had a strict training approach. He insisted that I memorize all the VHF VOR navigation stations along our route. He was impressed at how quickly I adapted to Gillette's operational style, and I felt like I was thriving in this new, highly professional environment.

One unintended consequence of flying the Gulfstream 1 was a slight hearing loss—a result of the extremely high-pitched noise generated by the combination of Rolls-Royce Dart turboprop engines and Dowty Propellers. That, combined with my prior exposure to flight deck noise on two separate carriers, took its toll. But it was worth it—I was living my aviation dream, flying a transport-category aircraft with seasoned professionals and learning at an accelerated pace.

The six months at Gillette went by in a flash. Soon, I found myself attending Gulfstream Initial Training at the FlightSafety Learning Center at LaGuardia Airport (LGA)—specifically, in the Marine Air Terminal, which housed FlightSafety Inc.'s only training center at the time.

When I entered the classroom, I looked for my name on the desk and noticed the name card next to mine. It read:

Wernher von Braun.

Yes, that Wernher von Braun—the former German rocket scientist, designer of the V-1 and V-2 rockets at Peenemünde, and father of the Saturn V rocket that would send men to the moon.

Von Braun, whom I simply addressed as "Wernher" (at his insistence), told me why he was in the class. As part of his postwar agreement with the U.S. government, once NASA purchased four Gulfstream 1s, he wanted to fly them himself. However, his German Private Pilot License (PPL) only had a glider endorsement.

NASA agreed, but only under the condition that he complete formal training and certification in the G-159 Gulfstream 1.

Wernher ended up being my simulator partner, though these 1960s-era simulators were nothing like the ones we have today. These early simulators:

- Did not move
- Had no visual displays
- Relied on analog dials that we twisted manually

It was primitive compared to today's Level-D flight simulators, but it got the job done.

At the end of the course, we went our separate ways.

Wernher returned to NASA in Alabama, continuing his work on the Saturn rocket program, while I returned home to Quincy, Massachusetts, moving back in with my parents to aggressively conduct a job search.

Thankfully, I had my MGB-GT transported back by my future brother-in-law, Ciro D'Angelo, so I at least had wheels while planning my next move.

Wernher, as he insisted I call him, explained why he was in the class. As part of his arrangement with the U.S. government, once NASA purchased four Gulfstream 1s, he wanted to fly them himself. The only issue? He only had a German Private Pilot License (PPL), and it was limited to gliders.

NASA agreed to his request—on the condition that he complete formal training and qualification in the G-159 Gulfstream 1.

Wernher became my simulator partner, but these simulators were nothing like the high-tech versions of today. These early training devices had:

- No motion capabilities
- No visual displays
- Only analog dials that we had to twist manually to simulate different flight conditions

It was a far cry from the modern Level-D Flight Simulation Devices (FSDs), but it served its purpose.

At the end of the course, we parted ways—Wernher returned to NASA in Alabama to continue his work on the Saturn rocket program, while I returned to Quincy, Massachusetts, moving back in with my parents to begin an aggressive job search.

Thankfully, I had my MGB-GT transported back by my future brother-in-law, Ciro D'Angelo, so I at least had wheels while figuring out my next move.

8
FLIGHT 08R

All dressed up as a Learjet 25 pilot—and actually had someplace to go! I also enjoyed the nickname "Lennie Learjet," which was bestowed upon me by "Smokey" Bennett, the Chief Pilot of Xerox Corporation, operating out of Hangar G.

In late 1968, I took a job as a CFI-A&I instructor for the famous lawyer F. Lee Bailey at his FBO, Marshfield Aviation, in Marshfield, Massachusetts.

Bailey wasn't just a high-profile attorney—he was also an Enstrom Helicopter dealer. He even had a private helipad in Marshfield Hills, where he would land and then pull his helicopter straight into his garage after a flight.

At Marshfield Aviation, I had plenty of veteran students taking advantage of the G.I. Bill to earn their Instrument Flight Rules (IFR) rating. We had a nicely configured Cessna 207, which made instrument training efficient.

Whenever I scheduled an IFR cross-country training flight, which was a required curriculum item, I would often recommend Westchester County Airport (HPN) as our destination.

That wasn't by accident.

Back then, HPN was the number one corporate aircraft-based airport—which meant prime opportunities for someone like me looking to break into business aviation.

So, while my students got valuable IFR cross-country experience, I used the lunch breaks at HPN to conduct job interviews with corporate flight departments.

It turned out to be one of the best career moves I ever made.

One of those interviews was with Jack Doswell—the namesake of the NBAA Life Achievement Award—and Chief Pilot of a brand-new Learjet 25. He was establishing a new flight department for American Standard and needed a copilot and Supervisor of Maintenance for their newly acquired Learjet.

I got the job.

I was officially hired as Director of Maintenance and Copilot for American Standard's Learjet 25.

At only 29 years old, my job at American Standard was my first real pilot opportunity, and I was Jack Doswell's first additional pilot in the newly established flight department.

Jack and I hit it off immediately. As the young, low-time pilot, I was lucky to be assigned to most of the jet flights, and I made the most of the opportunity.

Starting in 1969, while flying for American Standard, I

managed to fly to all 49 U.S. states (I missed Hawaii), every Canadian province, Bermuda, and most Central American states. Bermuda was a unique challenge due to its strict landing regulations for corporate aircraft, making it an achievement in itself.

I also got a taste of flying in Europe, thanks to Captain Company, who operated a Learjet 24 under American Standard's "Ideal Standard" brand.

Jack was a tremendous mentor. As the junior pilot, I was averaging 600–650 hours per year, which rapidly built my experience. Jack became like a father to me, opening doors that would help shape my career.

I remember how much respect I had for him when he invited me over to his house on the night of July 20, 1969, to watch the lunar landing live. It was a surreal moment—watching Neil Armstrong's first steps on the moon while sitting beside a mentor who had already changed my life in so many ways.

Not long after, a highly experienced Learjet pilot, Dave N., joined our team.

Dave was already type-rated in the Lear, but what made him unique was his experience flying historic aircraft like the Ford Trimotor 5 and Boeing 247. He had flown for Port Clinton Airways, transporting school children off Port Clinton, Ohio, during the winter months. He once told me how he sometimes had to navigate by the cracks in the ice on Lake Erie—a reminder of how much flying has evolved over the decades.

I rotated between flying with Jack and Dave, gaining valuable experience from both. But nothing could prepare me for the challenge we were about to face on a winter company trip from HPN to Cleveland Hopkins Airport (CLE).

We took off from HPN with three passengers and a full fuel load, bound for CLE. As we neared Cleveland, Lake Erie's infamous lake effect weather began to rapidly deteriorate. The airport was still open, but conditions worsened so quickly that we were put into a holding pattern, awaiting clearance to land on Runway 23L (Back Course ILS)—with blowing snow and strong crosswinds making the approach even more challenging.

Upon arrival at the holding fix, we were number ten in a

stack of commercial and corporate aircraft. We estimated we could hold for about 20 minutes before we would have to divert to our alternate, but then, things took a turn for the worse.

One by one, aircraft ahead of us were attempting approaches —some making it in, others executing missed approaches due to whiteout conditions. Then, it was our turn.

We prepared the cockpit for the Back Course ILS approach to Runway 23L, following all standard procedures. The approach lights were operational, and we were hopeful but prepared for the worst. As we descended toward minimums, I looked out the window and spotted the runway lights in sight.

"Runway in sight!" I called out.

A few seconds later, Dave looked up from the instruments to confirm, but in an instant, the runway environment disappeared into blowing snow. Neither of us could positively identify the runway.

Missed approach!

We both called for a go-around, and I immediately selected approach flaps and retracted the landing gear. That's when we realized something was very, very wrong. As we climbed out, my scan of the cockpit instruments revealed two crucial warning indicators:

1. "LOW HYD PRESSURE" on the Master Caution Panel
2. Zero hydraulic pressure on the system gauge

Our flaps weren't retracting, and our gear retraction was sluggish. At that point, Dave was fully focused on executing the missed approach, while I analyzed our system failures. We advised ATC that we were declaring an emergency.

At the time, all major airports along Lake Erie, Michigan, and Ontario were experiencing conditions at or below IFR minimums. Our alternate airport was Burke Lakefront Airport (BKL), but even that had intermittent clouds at 1,000 feet, strong crosswinds, and no braking action due to ice-covered runways.

With few options left, we decided that we would have to lower the landing gear manually using the emergency pneumatic system, but only at the last possible moment before landing to conserve fuel. There was no way to retract the gear once it was deployed—it would be locked down for good.

When the gear was finally lowered, the cockpit became deafeningly loud. Unlike today, we weren't wearing headsets, and the increased drag meant we had to fly at higher-than-normal approach speeds since we had no hydraulically operated flaps.

The approach controller's voice had changed. We could hear the concern in his tone as we were vectored back to attempt another Back Course ILS approach to Runway 23L—this time, with no second chances.

Fuel remaining was becoming a crucial factor as we listened intently to our next ATC approach instructions. We were heading on a radar vector of about 090 degrees, which seemed odd for an approach to 23L. Then came a call from ATC that changed everything:

"N270AS, turn right to 240 degrees to intercept the ILS approach for Runway 27."

This was a surprise. We were fully configured for a 23L Back Course approach, and now ATC was vectoring us to a different runway. We immediately asked ATC to confirm, and they did—but with one major caveat: Runway 27 had not been plowed and had two feet of snow with possible icy conditions.

There was no time to argue. We complied with ATC's vectoring and quickly adapted to the new situation. The only positive element of this change was that the winds were blowing 20-30 knots from 270 degrees, meaning that while the runway was covered in snow, at least we would be landing into a strong headwind, which could help slow us down. Luckily, we still had electric nosewheel steering, which meant we had some control after landing.

ATC also informed us that they could provide a Ground Controlled Approach (GCA) if necessary. As we got closer to the airport, we started to make ground contact through the snow and saw the lead-in lights to Runway 27. The sun had just begun to set, and as we descended, we could make out roughly half of the 6,000-foot runway through the snow cover.

We quickly briefed our landing strategy. Given the risk of sliding on an unplowed surface, we decided to shut down both engines once we crossed the threshold and had solid contact with the runway surface, minimizing any unwanted forward motion.

The touchdown felt like jumping onto pillows on a bed. The thick snow absorbed most of our energy, and our forward motion came to a stop much faster than expected. Once we were safely down, we restarted one engine to restore heat and lighting in the cabin.

Tower then informed us that it would be a while before they could tow us off the runway since all available plows were needed for the active runway.

From a pilot's standpoint, what Dave and I had just experienced was what we called an LCE—Life-Changing Event.

While waiting for the tow, we opened the onboard bar. Once everyone had settled, we began debriefing and analyzing everything that had just happened, making note of the lessons learned.

As a direct result of this event, we changed our cockpit procedures and communication habits:

- When ATC vectored us for an approach to a different runway than expected, we did not immediately acknowledge the change when checking in with the new controller. We should have confirmed the instructions the moment they were issued. Moving forward, we decided to always restate runway assignments. For example: *"Understand N720AS vectors to Runway 27 ILS?"* This small procedural change would ensure that we were always aware of exactly where ATC was directing us.

- Even when landing at an airport with only one runway, such as an island destination, we made it a habit to always include the runway number in our readbacks to avoid assumptions or miscommunication.

- A headset was now mandatory for both pilots during approaches and at any altitude below 10,000 feet. The cockpit noise from the emergency pneumatic landing gear extension had been so overwhelming that we had missed a critical ATC instruction. A headset would have prevented this.

- We committed to finding ways to increase our safety margins when flying under Severe Weather Aviation Procedures (SWAP). This meant adopting a more conservative approach in fuel planning, alternate selection, and weather diversions.

- And, most importantly, we vowed to always expect the unexpected.

We later had the opportunity to listen to the ATC tower tapes and hear the command we had missed. That moment confirmed what we already knew—our failure to acknowledge the change in approach runways was a direct result of cockpit noise interfering with critical communications.

This experience permanently changed the way I flew for the rest of my 50-plus-year career.

After this life-changing event, I wrote an article in *Flight Operations* magazine to share our experience and offer ideas to prevent what happened to us through new habit patterns and improved cockpit resource management (CRM) procedures.

At the time, we didn't have a formal *Safety Management System (SMS)* like what is now required by FAR 121 operations, but we spent a lot of time thinking about how to develop the framework for one.

One particularly memorable trip was when we flew to a Del Monte banana farm/plantation in Puerto Limón, Costa Rica, where our company president had an interest in visiting. Upon landing, we were given instructions to park at the approach end of the runway because a C-46 from San José was scheduled to arrive shortly to pick up a load of bananas.

From there, we had to take a Cessna 185 from a makeshift jungle runway, something that left me uneasy. The bush pilot, however, assured us he knew what he was doing. Jack asked me to sit in the front seat since I had significant Cessna 180 experience—except for one crucial difference: the control wheel on the right front seat was missing, removed to lighten the aircraft's weight for carrying a higher load in the humid conditions.

We made it out safely, but as soon as we returned to the main airport, we fired up the Learjet and headed straight for Mexico City, shaking our heads at what had just happened.

Then there was a truly terrifying event about two years into my tenure with American Standard.

Jack Doswell and I were flying out west to Salt Lake City, Utah, and Rock Springs, Wyoming, with a stop at the Learjet factory in Wichita to check on the status of our newly ordered Learjet 25B. This was just after Jack had returned from a vacation in Barbados.

During the trip, Jack started experiencing intestinal problems, and I began noticing small changes in his physical condition. At first, it was subtle—he had trouble squeezing the Push-to-Talk (PTT) button on the hand mic. Then, at the Learjet factory in Wichita, his symptoms worsened. He had to use the restroom frequently, and his overall strength and coordination seemed to be deteriorating.

By the time we were on our final leg back to Westchester County Airport (KHPN), his condition had noticeably declined. His ability to talk and move in his seat became concerning.

I asked Jack if we should divert and get him checked out, but he refused, insisting we press on since we were only 30 minutes from landing.

After touching down at HPN, we taxied to Hangar C-1,

where Don Archibald, our new Director of Maintenance (DOM), was waiting for us.

Jack had difficulty getting out of the cockpit, and I could see he was struggling. I tried to help him into our office, as it was already late at night. I offered to drive him home, but Jack, stubborn as ever, insisted on calling his wife, Marian, to take a taxi to White Plains Airport to pick him up. He didn't want to drive, but he also didn't want anyone else to take him home.

As he filled out the flight log, I noticed something that alarmed me even more—he could barely press the pencil hard enough to make an indent on the paper.

I insisted on driving him home, but he refused again, telling me to rest up for my early morning flight to Pittsburgh Allegheny County Airport (AGC) with our first contract copilot.

I mentioned my concerns to Don, and thankfully, he stepped in and offered to take Jack home. That made me feel a little better, but something in my gut told me that something was seriously wrong.

I flew my trip the next day, and as soon as I landed at AGC, I called the office to talk to our secretary, Audrey Bair, but she wasn't there. I tried calling the flight operations department that shared our hangar (RCA, Jim Mandel and company), but they weren't available either. Something in my gut told me something was wrong.

On a hunch, I called Greenwich Hospital and asked for the emergency room. The doctor in charge confirmed they had a patient by the name of Jack Doswell, but he wasn't available to talk. That's when I asked to speak to his wife, Marian.

As I waited for her to come to the phone, I started wondering if their recent vacation in Barbados had anything to do with his sudden health decline.

When Marian finally answered, I asked how Jack was doing.

"Not good," she said. "They don't even know how to diagnose his condition."

She told me that Jack couldn't talk and had lost all mobility. In essence, he was paralyzed from his nose to his toes.

Marian was too upset to keep talking, so I asked to speak

with the doctor attending to Jack. I explained that I had been flying with him just hours before and asked if his condition could be contagious—whether I needed to be quarantined.

The doctor's response was far from reassuring.

"We don't know what he has, and we don't know if it's contagious."

Jack was transferred to ICU, where doctors eventually determined that he had all the symptoms of Guillain-Barré Syndrome (GBS)—a rare disorder in which the immune system attacks the body's nerves. They still weren't entirely sure, but at least they were starting to pinpoint a direction.

That didn't do much to ease my own concerns. I had been sitting right next to Jack for hours, breathing the same air, and I had no idea whether I had been exposed to something life-threatening. To this day, over 50 years later, I have never experienced any symptoms of Guillain-Barré Syndrome. Thank God.

Jack remained in ICU for quite some time, requiring round-the-clock care from a team of specialists.

One of his closest friends, J. Sheldon "Torch" Lewis, developed an alpha-numeric communication chart so that Jack could communicate through blinking—one blink for "no" and two blinks for "yes."

That simple system revealed something critical.

Through blinking, Jack was able to tell us that his night nurse wasn't turning him over properly, leading to severe bed rashes and sores.

That nurse was immediately fired.

Through intense physical therapy, Jack gradually started regaining strength and movement. Though Guillain-Barré is still not well understood, doctors have since identified possible triggers, including Campylobacter bacteria (found in uncooked poultry) and certain influenza viruses.

I have counted my blessings every day that I was not affected, but I remain acutely aware of any physical changes that remind me of what I witnessed while flying with Jack.

Against all odds, Jack recovered.

With perseverance, he regained his FAA Medical Certificate, earned additional type ratings, and even completed an MBA.

Jack set an example for pilots and professionals who have faced serious health challenges and still wanted to continue their careers.

His legacy in aviation was so significant that the NBAA dedicated its prestigious "Life Achievement Award" in his name—an award given to individuals who have exemplified resilience and dedication to aviation despite seemingly insurmountable challenges.

As the last pilot to fly with Jack in American Standard's Lear 25 before he began showing symptoms of Guillain-Barré Syndrome, I will never forget him or the impact he had on my career in business aviation.

Jack was more than a mentor—he was a guiding force who helped shape my future, teaching me lessons about professionalism, resilience, and leadership that I carried with me for the rest of my career.

After writing this section about Jack, I was contacted by a long-time friend, Dave Hurley, who shared some anecdotes about our enduring friendship and Jack's influence on both of our careers.

I am thankful and grateful that Dave has allowed me to share those stories with you.

9

FLIGHT 09L

1970-1980s

On May 30, 1970, Elli and I were married at Our Lady of Good Counsel Church in Staten Island, near the ferry entrance. The ceremony was conducted by a very Irish priest, and after a lively and memorable "Look of Love" reception, we set off the next day for a three-week honeymoon filled with unexpected moments.

One of the first surprises came early in our trip. On our first night in London, the hotel maid unexpectedly opened our door the next morning, took one look at us, and said, *"Sorry, I didn't mean to awaken your father."*

That set the tone for the rest of our honeymoon.

We began by flying KLM Airlines to Amsterdam and then traveled aboard American Standard's Learjet 24, which was registered in Switzerland but based in Brussels, Belgium. Our pilots for the trip were Captain Claude Compan, a charismatic Frenchman, and Co-Captain Gerry Schoenfeld, a former Belgian Rafael fighter pilot. Both were fascinating characters in their own right.

Elli and I met them at the Excelsior Hotel in Brussels, conveniently located near the Grand Palace. From there, we were flown to Zurich and Barcelona, occasionally sharing the aircraft with American Standard executives. Fortunately, they didn't seem to mind that we were on our honeymoon, which made the experience even more enjoyable.

During our stay in Zurich, Switzerland, we enjoyed a classic fondue dinner, accompanied by a few "adult beverages." However, the next morning, Elli wasn't feeling great.

That's when our ever-resourceful French captain, Claude, came to the rescue.

He turned to Elli and said, *"Elenor, you sit up front near the cockpit, and you will feel like you are flying the jet. That will make you feel better! And, we will even give you a beautiful yellow Learjet hat to make you feel even happier!"*

Sure enough, with Captain Elli seated near the cockpit, she began to feel better. With a little guidance from Claude and Gerry, she even got to "fly" us to Brussels.

We came in a little fast over the runway threshold, but everything was well under control. Captain Elli even got credit for the landing—though, somehow, when we tell this story, we always seem to forget to mention that little detail.

We spent the next couple of days in Brussels, staying at the Excelsior Hotel, which was walking distance from the Grand Palace. Every night, we visited the same café, where we befriended a French entertainer with a beautiful voice and a talent for playing the guitar.

After a few glasses of wine, we found ourselves singing along to *"Ooh Champs-Élysées, Ooh Champs-Élysées"*—a song that, to this day, instantly brings back memories of that magical time.

Looking back on our honeymoon, we had no formal travel plans—no hotel bookings, no pre-planned excursions. We simply let the trip unfold. Our most expensive hotel bill was a mere $17 USD per night, and the only parking we did in Paris was on the sidewalks.

By the time we left, we had racked up 17 parking violation tickets, which we casually stuffed into the glove compartment.

Somehow, we never had to pay a single one.

It must have been a French wedding gift!

After enjoying Brussels and Zurich, we boarded our beautiful Learjet and headed for Barcelona, Spain, with a full and diverse complement of people on board.

Among us were a French pilot, a Belgian pilot, two Americans (one who spoke Italian), a secretary from the UK with a strong accent, and a Flemish-speaking passenger. I mention all of these ethnic backgrounds because, in a strange way, they all played a role in what could have been an event-changing moment.

I was driving a rental car from the hotel to the airport, where our airplane was hangared, when we were suddenly pulled over by a motorcycle cop. I handed him my Connecticut driver's license, and before I could say anything, everyone in the car started talking at once.

One passenger spoke in Flemish, another in English, Elli in Italian, Claude in French, and me in Bostonian. The poor Spanish cop looked completely overwhelmed, stared at us for a moment, then suddenly turned off his motorcycle's rotating beacon, waved his hands in frustration, and shouted:

"AEROPUERTO! AEROPUERTO!"

And with that, we were free to go—miraculously with no moving violations!

We obviously had some fun along the way. But our private Learjet adventures were coming to an end. The last week of our honeymoon was spent in Naples, Italy—Elli's hometown—where her relatives were thrilled to have us staying with them. That week, however, was not without its memorable moments.

One night, we went out to a disco club—you remember those, don't you? Elli's cousin, who was a graduate student, joined us, and after a while, we got caught up in the music, the energy, and the excitement of the night. At some point, we lost track of her cousin.

We searched everywhere, checking the places we thought she might be, but with no luck. With no other choice, we headed back to Elli's aunt's home, where we were staying, assuming she would turn up. The next morning, we woke up to Elli's aunt screaming—in Italian. We quickly learned why.

Elli's cousin had left in the middle of the night because she had experienced a calling—a deep spiritual awakening—and had joined a convent of Cloister Nuns. Not just any nuns. Cloistered nuns. That meant no talking. No outside contact. Nothing.

Since my Italian was marginal at best, I had to rely entirely on Elli for direction on what to do next. But the truth was, there was nothing we could do. Her cousin was an intelligent adult who had made a deliberate, spiritual choice. Eventually, the family came to accept her decision, and we wrapped up our honeymoon with a trip to Milan before flying back to JFK on a KLM stretched DC-8.

10

FLIGHT 10R

In early 1974, the importance of time management became a major focus for me as I approached the point where I needed to matriculate in order to complete my MBA at Iona College. After much discussion with my thesis advisor, Dr. Ted Schwartz, I initially proposed a topic that I was genuinely passionate about:

"The Use of Corporate Aircraft as an Instrument of Marketing Persuasion in the Sale of Industrial Products."

Unfortunately, my proposal was rejected.It was deemed outside the realm of an MBA curriculum, as it was considered more appropriate for a doctoral dissertation.

Dr. Schwartz, who was not only head of the department but also a Senior Vice President for Marketing at General Foods, personally disagreed with the concept of using corporate aircraft for marketing purposes. He refused to endorse my thesis because he simply didn't believe in it. Reluctantly, I pivoted to a different topic:

"Time Management and Its Relative Impact on the Executive."

The challenge now was finding research material. I searched everywhere, starting with the Baker Library at Harvard's Cambridge campus, but I found nothing useful.

During an Easter weekend trip to Boca Raton in 1974, I visited the Florida Atlantic University library and managed to locate a few references, but it still wasn't enough. Then, in what felt like divine intervention, I stumbled upon a game-changing discovery while flying on United Airlines to San Francisco.

I was reading Hemispheres magazine when I came across an article about Alan Lakein's book, "How to Control Your Time and Your Life." That was it. As soon as I landed, I rushed to find a payphone (no cell phones back then) and called Alan Lakein's office in downtown San Francisco. His secretary, Sally Roper-Scales (a name I'll never forget), answered the phone.

I introduced myself, explained that I was an MBA candidate researching time management, and asked if I could meet Mr. Lakein for a few minutes to ask some questions. She paused the call, then came back and said, "Okay, Mr. Lakein can meet you later today—for five minutes." I made sure not to waste a second of that opportunity.

It was a short but valuable conversation, and I assured Mr. Lakein that I would credit him in my thesis. When the time came to present my thesis to my peers at Iona, I earned an A+ from Dr. Schwartz. In an ironic twist, after reading my thesis and hearing my argument, Dr. Schwartz admitted that he had changed his stance on corporate aircraft use.

He now believed that corporate aviation could be an effective marketing tool and advocated for its use at General Foods. That A+ secured my full matriculation, and I officially graduated with my MBA.

We have a saying in Scituate, and it has become my motto in life:

"Don't Ever Give Up If You Believe in Yourself."

Or, as we say at sea:

"Don't Give Up the Ship—Ever!"

11
FLIGHT 11L

In 1977, I was commissioned to help a client in the Republic of South Africa (RSA) find a turboprop aircraft for his diamond mining operation.

He was considering purchasing a Cessna 441 Conquest, but before making a decision, he called me to confirm whether a U.S. FAA Airworthiness Directive (AD)—which had grounded the C-441 due to a faulty elevator trim actuator—would apply if the aircraft were registered under the ZS RSA state registry. After researching the FAA bilateral agreement with RSA, I found that the AD would still apply, meaning the aircraft would be affected regardless of registration.

I recommended a Rockwell 690B instead, equipped with slipper tanks (adding an extra 120 gallons of fuel) and a Very Low Frequency (VLF) navigation system—a technology also used on U.S. submarines for long-range navigation. This would provide greater reliability and avoid the ongoing AD issue with the Cessna 441.

He agreed to purchase the Rockwell 690B, with the added condition that I train his two RSA pilots—Mel Colyn and another former RSA Air Force pilot—for their U.S. FAA ATP license.

Mel Colyn had already made quite the unconventional impression on the principal of the diamond mine before I even arrived. He had built and flown his own Pitts Special aerobatic aircraft to the remote mining camp, landing on a makeshift runway. To demonstrate his airmanship, he performed an aerobatic routine for the mine owner.

That sealed the deal, and he was hired on the spot.

We attended Rockwell Turboprop School in Oklahoma and completed flight training before arranging for their U.S. ATP check rides with the Boston FSDO. With the pilots certified, we began planning our 9,000-mile ferry flight to South Africa, which would take approximately 42.5 hours of flight time.

Our route from Boston took us through:

- Goose Bay, Canada (CYYR)
- Reykjavik, Iceland (BIRK)
- Paris, France (LFPB) for the first 100-hour inspection
- Seville, Spain (LEZL)
- Las Palmas, Canary Islands (GCLP)—a last-minute change from Tenerife due to the tragic Boeing 747 collision between KLM and Pan Am that had occurred just weeks earlier, killing 583 people
- Abidjan, Ivory Coast (DIAP)
- Kinshasa, Zaire (FZAA)
- Bulawayo, Rhodesia (FUJN)
- Rand Airport (FAGM), Johannesburg, South Africa

As we stopped for a tech stop in Kinshasa, we were alerted to an escalating conflict ahead called the Kolwezi Offensive. This was a military operation by French and Belgian airborne forces in May 1978, launched in response to an invasion by FLNC rebels who had seized control of Kolwezi, Zaire. The mission aimed to rescue European and Zairean hostages held by the rebels.

We received intelligence from a Pan Am Boeing 707 crew, who gave us updated information on the security situation. Despite the growing tensions, we decided to proceed cautiously. After four hours of flying, we determined that it would be safer to land in Bulawayo, Rhodesia (FUJN), which both Mel and the other RSA pilot agreed would be a secure location for the night.

At 2:30 AM RSA time, we landed at Bulawayo Airport, where we were met by a pleasant customs and immigration officer—an RSA citizen nearing retirement. After completing our formalities, we thanked him with a small token of appreciation, which he graciously accepted. We were one step closer to our final destination in Johannesburg.

The next morning, I had my first South African breakfast—a sunny-side-up ostrich egg, and I have to say, it was delicious! Shortly after, we drove to the airport for the final leg of this fascinating journey through hidden runways, heading to Rand Airport (FAGM).

Upon arrival, we offloaded our precious cargo, which included:

- Day-glow orange golf balls for golfing in the Kalahari Desert (which also turned out to be an effective hair removal tool!)
- Hard-to-find luxury items that weren't easily available in South Africa at the time.
- The next month brought a series of unique flying experiences, including stops in:
- Windhoek, Namibia, where we ran into Telly Savalas (yes, *Kojak* himself!) at the Hansa Beer Brewery
- Kimberley, RSA, home to the world's largest diamond mine, owned by Anglo-American DeBeers—the same company Mel used to work for, transporting "goods"
- Mozambique, Botswana, Swakopmund (Namibia), Pretoria, and Cape Town

One flight that stood out was when we picked up a load of South African lobsters, and just before departing, I received a call from my daughter. She asked, "Daddy, are you going to be home for my dance recital this weekend?" That was all I needed to hear. I immediately made arrangements to leave as soon as possible, making sure to sign Mel as PIC along with his copilot for the owner's approval before heading back home.

During the late 1980s, I was blessed to fly two Challenger jets on contract assignments, both of which took me to some incredible destinations.

But these weren't just any Challengers. Each of them had a medallion in the cockpit, marking them as something special.

The first Challenger I flew had an event that made me truly believe in divine intervention. This particular Challenger was one of two that had been blessed by Pope John Paul II—and had the Papal Medallions in the cockpit to prove it. In a way, I suppose you could say we were flying with a little extra insurance on every flight.

One particular flight out of a remote airfield in western Pennsylvania en route to Atlanta still gives me chills.

We had just leveled off at FL390 (39,000 feet) when I looked out the window and saw an unidentified object. A few seconds later, I realized it wasn't moving away from us—it was staying in the same position relative to the window. *That meant we were on a collision course.*

It turned out to be a weather balloon, roughly 15+ feet in diameter, depending on its sensor package. Trailing from the balloon was a 50-foot-long tethered cable, carrying a radiosonde package for atmospheric data collection. These balloons can reach altitudes of over 100,000 feet.

A quick glance at the IRS (Inertial Reference System) confirmed that it was closing in at a 90-degree angle at approximately 150 knots. We had seconds to react.

I immediately executed an evasive maneuver to the left, banking just enough to avoid a potential disaster. Once we found enough separation, we reported the near-collision to ATC.

Their response?

They had no idea it was even there.

The controller explained that the weather balloon didn't have a transponder, nor any tracking system that would allow it to be visible on their radar scopes. That realization sparked discussions about how to prevent future catastrophic incidents involving these objects.

Looking back, I can't help but wonder—was it pure luck that we spotted the balloon in time, or was it the blessing of that

Pope's medallion in the cockpit? Either way, it was a flight I would never forget.

We landed safely in Atlanta, and after securing the aircraft, I took the time to explain to our passengers why we had to make an evasive maneuver early in the flight.

Thankfully, the maneuver had been smooth enough that most of them hadn't even realized anything unusual had happened—but once they heard the story, they were fascinated and a little shocked.

For those interested, here's a link to information on the Global Weather Balloon Program, which continues to operate beyond any control or awareness of pilots in flight:

https://www.nasa.gov/scientificballoons/

Aside from the divine intervention of avoiding that balloon, this aircraft itself was special in another way. The owner of the Challenger was originally from Florence, Italy, and he had designed the aircraft's interior as a tribute to his hometown. The rear bulkhead featured a stunning fabric depiction of the Ponte Vecchio bridge spanning the Arno River. To complement this masterpiece, the entire cabin floor—from the rear bulkhead to the cockpit—was covered in custom carpet that replicated the flow of the Arno River. It was a flying work of art—something you wouldn't expect to find in a high-performance jet cruising at 39,000 feet.

Every time I stepped into that cabin, it felt as if I were walking across the Arno itself—a true testament to the owner's love for Florence and Italian craftsmanship.

12

FLIGHT 12R

Circa 1980-1990s

Corporate Flight Operations

My first large flight department experience came when I was recruited to be Chief Pilot for Connecticut General, which was in the process of merging with Insurance Company of North America (INA). The result of that merger was CIGNA, a multi-billion-dollar insurance company with an expanding aviation division.

From 1980 to 1988, I was fully consumed with CIGNA's flight operations, managing a growing fleet and ensuring the company's aviation activities aligned with its corporate objectives. Professionally, the move was an excellent financial decision, but like any demanding career shift, there were compromises. Looking back, while the professional gains were substantial, I may not have always made the best choices when balancing work with the needs of my wife and family.

Managing a large flight department is never without challenges, but I found that things ran relatively smoothly. When CIGNA decided that its corporate shuttle was no longer needed, we made sure the affected pilots were offered additional training in the two aircraft they operated, ensuring they had continued career opportunities. Other personnel were similarly accommodated to minimize disruption to their professional paths.

At its peak, the CIGNA fleet included:

- Two Sikorsky S-76 helicopters
- One Westwind medium jet
- One Challenger 601
- One Gulfstream-1, which served as the company's corporate shuttle, configured for 18 passengers and operating two round trips per day between Bradley (BDL) and Philadelphia (PHL)

There were several milestones during my time at CIGNA that significantly enhanced my career.

One major accomplishment was FAA certifying the first corporate IAI Westwind aircraft and crews for Category 2 (CAT 2) approach standards. This certification process was already under consideration before I joined as Chief Pilot, initiated by a consultant who had argued that CAT 2 certification would improve safety. However, I wasn't entirely convinced by this argument. Given that I was working for a major insurance company, I wanted to be sure that the additional investment in training, equipment, and calibration was justified beyond a shadow of a doubt.

At the time, there were 52 airports in the U.S. that allowed CAT 2 instrument approaches. Of those, CIGNA had business offices near about half of them, meaning our aircraft occasionally had reason to operate in those areas. If you factor in the number of days and nights when these airports experienced weather conditions below CAT 1 minimums (200-foot ceiling and 1/2-mile visibility), we had to determine whether a CAT 2 certification was practically necessary or simply an expensive luxury.

The decision wasn't just about the cost of equipment—it was about operational strategy. If a flight crew was approaching a destination in CAT 2 conditions, should they:

- Proceed with the approach, trusting in their training and the aircraft's CAT 2 capability?
- Hold and wait for the weather to improve?
- Divert to another airport altogether, avoiding the risk of attempting the approach?

There was also the critical issue of control tower reliability. If the CAT 2 monitoring device in the air traffic control tower (CAB) was inoperative, pilots would be prevented from executing a CAT 2 approach altogether, making the entire certification process potentially moot in certain situations.

Beyond the technical side of flight operations, I introduced an organizational behavior tool that I had learned about while earning my MBA at Iona College. It was called an Organizational Climate Questionnaire/Survey, developed by the Boston-based think tank McBer.

I modified the survey, tailoring it to focus on enhancing overall safety and improving operational efficiency within our flight department. The results were remarkable:

- Zero personnel turnover during my tenure
- Improved communication and team cohesion
- Performance bonuses awarded at the end of the year for both flying and non-flying personnel

Implementing this structured feedback process not only improved safety but also fostered a stronger, more committed flight department team.

Looking back, my time at CIGNA was a formative period in my career, demonstrating that managing a corporate flight department requires much more than just flying skills—it demands strategic planning, personnel management, and a deep understanding of organizational behavior.

13
FLIGHT 13L

The 1980s were a time of transition for our family. Our kids were no longer just growing up—they were moving on to college and beginning their own journeys.

Cristina attended Stonehill College outside of Boston and later participated in an exchange program at Richmond College in London, which led to an unexpected and unforgettable travel experience. Marc attended Wentworth Institute, where he worked diligently and ultimately graduated Summa Cum Laude in 1994.

When Cristina was preparing for her exchange student assignment in London (and Paris, too), she expressed some concerns about her flight on Air India. She called me, asking whether the airline was safe. To reassure her, I reached out to my colleagues at the Flight Safety Foundation to check for any potential issues.

The only complaint I could find wasn't about safety at all—it was from the flight attendants, who were frustrated about having to fold the blankets after each flight. I passed this amusing detail along to Cristina, telling her she had nothing to worry about. The next day, after she had arrived safely in London, we got a call from her.

Cristina could hardly speak—her voice was filled with excitement and disbelief. Finally, after catching her breath, she said,

"You're not going to believe what happened on our flight." Thinking the worst but hoping for the best, I asked what had happened. She said, "We were all seated in the economy section, and we were surrounded by Mother Teresa and about 20 other nuns!" I was stunned.

It was hard to believe, but it was true—our daughter had been blessed with the presence of Mother Teresa herself on her flight to London. We will forever be grateful and thankful that Cristina not only had a safe journey with Air India but also experienced something truly divine along the way.

14
FLIGHT 14R

As part of my role at a large insurance company, I was invited to attend the 38th International Air Safety Seminar, held from November 4-7, 1985, in Boston, Massachusetts. The seminar focused on the *Influence of Training, Operational, and Maintenance Practices on Flight Safety*. At the time, I was serving as Deputy Chairman of the Americas Corporate Advisory Committee for the Flight Safety Foundation. During the event, I delivered a white paper titled *The Practice, Philosophy, Underwriting Considerations, and Future of Extended Twin-Jet Over-Water Operations (ETOPS)*. This survey aimed to gauge industry perspectives on oceanic crossings with twin-engine aircraft versus four-engine aircraft, as well as the potential need for specialized insurance for both subsonic and supersonic flights.

My experience at the previous Flight Safety Foundation (FSF) conference led me to accept an invitation to attend a significant Battelle gathering in Dayton, Ohio, on *High-Speed Commercial Flight*. There, I had the good fortune of sitting next to Ben Rich, Director of Lockheed's legendary *Skunk Works (LMSW)*. Ben was intrigued by a wind tunnel model I was holding—a mockup of a Supersonic Business Jet (SSBJ) designed by an engineering group at Parks College of St. Louis University. The project, called the *Global Connector II*, was the focal point of my FSF ETOPS white paper.

(ADD: St. Louis Dispatch, February 10, 1986, which details how I contributed to the design of the student-led Supersonic Business Jet.)

Five years later, in 1991, I was on a Falcon 50 trip to Burbank, California. After landing and parking the aircraft, I was informed by the marshaller that I had a phone call waiting at the front desk—unexpected, as this was before cell phones were common. When I picked up the phone, I was surprised to hear Ben Rich on the other end. He told me he wanted to show me something and was sending a driver to pick me up.

At the time, *Skunk Works* was in the process of relocating its headquarters from Burbank to Palmdale, California (PMD), but they were still operating out of their secure, windowless offices. When I arrived at Ben's office, I saw a stunning model of what appeared to be a Small Supersonic Business Jet (SSBJ) sitting on his desk. It was a sleek, beautifully designed aircraft. Ben asked me what I thought, and after he shared some of its secret specifications, all I could say was—"Wow."

Our conversation remains confidential to this day. Before I left, Ben asked if I would keep in touch with him and the *Skunk Works* team. I agreed and ended up doing pro bono work for them for nearly a decade, until 1996. During that time, I worked closely with other *Skunk Works* directors, including Mike Evans, Rich Pollock, and Al Joerez (a former SR-71 pilot). My access continued until 1997, when my security badge expired.

In addition, I met with Captain Lowe, Director of Concorde Flight Training, who arranged for me and my students to "fly" the Concorde simulator. This happened just two weeks after *Rediffusion* installed its new *Day Visual* capability at the Filton facility in the UK.

As I left Ben's office that day, I couldn't quite believe the honor I had just experienced—being welcomed into one of the most renowned aerospace organizations in history. On our way out of the facility, as we reached the exit gate, I noticed a gentleman with a small stand displaying what appeared to be buckles. My curiosity got the best of me, and I asked the driver if I could approach him...

However, this wasn't just any ordinary individual—or kiosk.

The man was selling a *limited-edition* pewter belt buckle commemorating the historic SR-71 speed flight on March 6, 1990. That legendary flight began over Los Angeles International Airport (LAX) and concluded at Dulles International Airport (IAD), just outside Washington, D.C., where the aircraft would be permanently retired.

What made this flight extraordinary was its sheer speed—2,404 miles in just one hour and seven minutes! The SR-71, famously known as the *Blackbird*, maintained an average speed of 2,145 mph, setting an unbroken record for the fastest coast-to-coast flight. Today, that very aircraft rests at the *National Air and Space Museum's Steve F. Udvar-Hazy Center* Near Dulles Airport.

Naturally, I was intrigued by the belt buckle and asked if I could purchase one. The gentleman, however, informed me that they were exclusively available to LMSW employees. I explained that while I wasn't officially an LMSW employee, I had just come from a personal meeting with Ben Rich and had served as a *pro bono* consultant for *Skunk Works* for several years.

Hearing that, he immediately smiled and said, "Sure, that'll be $25."

Without hesitation, I handed over the money—the best $25 I've ever spent. Today, I proudly own *The Buckle Collection*, Made in the USA, serial number #633 of a limited edition of 2,112. For a pilot who has always revered aviation's greatest achievements, this buckle is more than just a piece of memorabilia—it's a cherished keepsake, one I hope to pass down to my son and grandsons.

15

FLIGHT 15L

A year later, as a guest of Captain Jock Lowe, I was fortunate enough to receive an upgrade on British Airways Concorde flight BA 001 from London Heathrow (LHR) to JFK. This wasn't just any flight—it marked the 15th anniversary of the highest-time Concorde airframe, which had logged over 15,000 flight hours.

Prior to this flight, I had traveled to Fornebu, Norway, to conduct FAR 61.58 Pilot in Command check rides for two Norwegian Challenger pilots in my role as a Designated Proficiency Pilot Examiner (PPE). I returned to Heathrow the same day, but thanks to jet lag (a brutal mix-up of circadian rhythms), I found myself unable to sleep the morning of my scheduled return to JFK.

Since my Boeing 747 flight wasn't until later that Sunday, I wandered into the Concorde lounge, passing time with a Mimosa in hand. Out of curiosity, I asked the concierge who would be piloting BA 001 that day. To my surprise, she responded, "Captain Jock Lowe."

I handed her my business card and asked if she could pass it along. She hesitated, explaining that a Dutch film crew was documenting this historic flight, and the captain was extremely busy. I thanked her for the effort and returned to my seat.

Then, about ten minutes later, after another Mimosa (or

two), she returned—this time holding a Concorde folio with my name assigned to seat 5A. You could have heard my cheer from London to NYC!

When I boarded, Captain Lowe greeted me at the entrance and, to my absolute astonishment, asked:

"Want to sit up front for takeoff?"

This was May 1991—a decade before 9/11, back when an invitation like this was still possible. Needless to say, I gratefully accepted.

I knew that, thanks to the Concorde's supersonic speeds, I would arrive in New York an hour before I left London—an aviation time-travel trick that never gets old. Our departure was at 10:30 AM LHR, with an estimated arrival at JFK of 9:30 AM.

Doing the math, I realized something incredible: *If everything went smoothly, I could surprise my wife and meet her and the kids at St. Mary's Church in Simsbury, Connecticut, before the 12:30 PM Catholic Mass ended!*

As we streaked across the Atlantic at Mach 2, the Concorde's airframe heated up, causing it to stretch by approximately eight inches—a quirk of supersonic flight. (Fun fact: The aisle floor is mounted on rollers to allow for this expansion.)

Of course, none of that stopped me from enjoying a five-course breakfast—partly at seat 5A, partly in the cockpit jump seat.

We touched down at JFK just after 9:30 AM, and I immediately raced to my car, determined to pull off my surprise reunion. I drove as fast as I could—responsibly, of course—and made it to Simsbury just in time.

As I slipped into our usual pew, I gently nudged my wife, Elli. She turned, startled, and whispered, "What are you doing here? You're not supposed to be home until late tonight!"

With a grin, I leaned in and replied:

"Honey, I missed you so much—I flew the Concorde home."

True story. And I've got the Mach Buster certificate, original crew signatures, Concorde playing cards, baggage tags, and—most importantly—a big smile to prove it. This remains one of my all-time favorite *Hidden Runway* stories, a tale I love sharing at aviation gatherings and cocktail parties.

Back in the early 1990s, I was flying for a Fortune 500 company on a trip to Mexico City, Mexico (MMMX). The flight from KHPN (Westchester County Airport) was uneventful. But things started to get interesting on the return leg via KDFW (Dallas/Fort Worth, TX), where we intended to clear U.S. Customs.

As we boarded our four passengers for departure—including the chairman of the company—they settled into their seats, and we completed our final preflight inspection. Everything was normal.

We ran through our pre-start checklist and began the engine start sequence. Engine #2 started normally. Then engine #3—also normal. But when we went to start engine #1... nothing. No movement of the starter. No lights. No sounds. No indication it was even attempting to start.

We turned to the abnormal checklist and began troubleshooting, but we couldn't find any obvious reason for the issue. Eventually, we shut down engines #2 and #3 and politely asked our passengers to return to the lounge while we worked to resolve the strange anomaly.

We placed calls to Garrett (the engine manufacturer) and Dassault (the airframe manufacturer), but neither provided a solution.

Then, my trusty co-captain, Dave Cassalia, brought up something interesting—and hard to believe.

Dave, a former door gunner and Army helo pilot in Vietnam, recalled a similar issue with an electric starter on a Huey. I asked him to explain further, and he said, "It's an easy fix... I think." He also mentioned he'd seen this same issue crop up on commercial aircraft.

Sometimes, in aviation, you have to improvise—think outside the box. This was one of those situations.

Dave said, "Here's what we did back then."

I should preface this by saying I had never once heard this

technique mentioned by any of our distinguished flight instructors, training organizations, or even the FAA.

Dave continued: "Get a rubber mallet and tap the starter case at about the 7 o'clock position—looking forward. That can shake the starter rotor off a 'flat spot,' allowing it to engage and complete the circuit."

Well, you should've seen the expression on the Mexican mechanic's face when we asked if he had a rubber mallet!

When he returned with one, I let Dave do the honors. He placed the mallet and gave it a precise tap at the right spot. Believe it or not, the starter engaged! I was in the cockpit, and I immediately continued the normal start procedure by moving the #1 throttle to idle. The engine started smoothly.

After checking all the gauges, everything looked good. With the "rubber mallet assist," we restarted engines #2 and #3. All three engines were running normally.

We reboarded our passengers, and I assured the chairman that the aircraft was operating safely and normally. I also explained that we'd request permission from Customs in Dallas to keep all three engines running during inspection—given the unusual circumstances. Thankfully, they agreed.

The rest of the flight went exactly as expected—normal.

When we arrived back at HPN, the chairman approached me and said, "Captain, looks like you'll need to carry a rubber mallet on all future flights!"

I responded, "Yes, sir! And by the way—you might want to consider whether you still need a mechanic."

16

FLIGHT 16R

In the 1980s, I was working for Dave Hurley's Flight Service Group (FSG), a FAR 135 charter company based out of Bridgeport, Connecticut. For one year, I was assigned to fly a CL-600 Challenger, an 18-passenger business jet, on tour with Jimmy Buffett (JB) and later with Jerry Garcia of the Grateful Dead (GD). Their schedules were uniquely demanding —two weeks on the road for JB's "Hot Water" tour, followed by a week off, then two to three weeks flying for the Grateful Dead

When I mentioned that Jimmy Buffett owned a Boeing, people's first reaction was always the same: *"Wow, he must be really rich!"* The reality? His Boeing was a Stearman biplane, a classic WWII-era training aircraft with two open cockpits—one for the instructor and one for the trainee.

One memorable JB flight began with a departure from San Francisco International Airport (SFO) to a small venue just south of the city. Jimmy asked if he could sit in the jump seat, and I gladly obliged. As we taxied out, I noticed that the nose wheel steering wasn't at 100%, but it was manageable as long as we could use asymmetric braking to steer—something that was FAA-approved under our Minimum Equipment List (MEL). With that in mind, we proceeded with the short 25-minute flight.

Takeoff was uneventful, and the landing gear retracted

normally. However, when we lowered the landing gear for approach, things took a turn. The nose gear extended—but the main gear remained stuck in the wheel wells.

Needless to say, JB was concerned. I reassured him that we had backup procedures and would get the main gear down. Rather than risk landing at a small venue airstrip, I made the decision to divert to Bakersfield, California (KBFL)—an airport with an 11,000-foot runway, which I knew well from my time stationed at NAS Lemoore.

En route to KBFL, we attempted our first emergency landing gear extension—and, thankfully, it worked perfectly. All three green indicator lights confirmed the gear was down, but on a Challenger, unlike the Falcon, we still needed to manually install gear pins to ensure all three were securely locked. Once we landed smoothly and cleared the runway, I personally installed the gear pins before proceeding any further.

With the aircraft safely on the ground, I turned to JB and asked, "Are you okay with flying back to the venue with the landing gear extended and locked?" The idea was to complete the show before heading to Oakland International Airport (OAK), where the aircraft could be properly repaired at Kaiser Air's hangar. After getting the green light from my boss, Smokey Bennett—a legendary former F-4 Phantom squadron skipper in the U.S. Navy—we made the call to the limousine company (on a landline, of course) and asked them to return to the venue.

With the landing gear extended for the entire flight, we actually arrived five minutes before the limo! Jimmy and his Coral Reefer Band still had plenty of time for a normal soundcheck before performing.

After the show, we flew to OAK, where we put the aircraft in the hangar. The technical crew soon diagnosed the issue—a failed nose gear control valve. Fortunately, a replacement part was available, but the repair turned out to be a real challenge—the valve was located in an awkward 7 o'clock position under the cockpit, making it difficult to remove and install.

By the next day, the aircraft was fully repaired, and we continued the tour without further incident. Looking back, we were incredibly lucky that our emergency procedures worked exactly as they should. A minor anomaly could have been a major problem—but instead, it became just another wild chapter in my aviation career.

On the final leg of the "Hot Water" tour, Jimmy Buffett asked if he could join me in the cockpit for a chat during our 5 ½-hour flight to Key West, Florida (EYW). He had invited Gracie, Ralph MacDonald, and JL Jamison as his guests, making for a relaxed and lively flight.

During our conversation, Jimmy excitedly shared that he had just purchased his first airplane, a Lake Renegade amphibian. After some classic "airplane talk," he mentioned that he wanted to earn his Instrument rating and asked if I was a CFI-I (Certified Flight Instructor - Instrument).

I told him I was, but since I didn't know when we'd cross paths again, we exchanged phone numbers and set a plan to train him in his Renegade, focusing on flying solely by instruments, particularly when taking off from water and navigating controlled airspace.

Our Flight Service Group (FSG) charter crew were all musically inclined and massive Parrot Heads. In honor of our time flying with JB, we wrote a song titled "707" or "We'd Fly"—a fun aviation-themed tribute to Buffett.

Lyrics to "707" (We'd Fly):

> We'd fly in a 707, right up to Heaven,
> We'd fly in a DC-8, to the Golden Gate,
> We'd take a Constellation, all over the nation,
> Just to see you, Jimmy, just to see you!
> We'd take an SST, wherever you wander,
> Or a DC-3, or Curtis Condor,
> We'd fly a Jet Crusader, to the Equator,
> Just to see you, Jimmy, just to see you!
> We'd go to the Moon, in a space capsule,
> If you could fit us into your schedule,
> We'd take a CANADAIR, through the air,
> Just to see you, Jimmy, just to see you!

> We'd fly in a 707, right up to Heaven,
> Take a flying saucer, or a PBY,
> We'd take a Grumman Mallard, to hear your ballads,
> Just to see you-hoo-hoo, just to see you!
> *I even added my own lyrics:*
> Because of you, Jimmy, we'd fly the world,
> It would be fun to do it with you in a Grumman Mallard or PBY—why?
> Just to see you, you-hoo, Jimmy,
> Just to BE with you-hoo-hoo-hoo!

The original song sheet with lyrics was produced by Smokey, Jeannie, Bob, and me.

I don't know if this song ever made its way to JB, but now that he has passed on, I think it would be a worthy addition to his legacy. If the original authors are still around, they might consider sharing it in his honor.

For over a decade, Jimmy and I kept in touch, yet our schedules never quite aligned to make the instrument training happen. Fate, however, had its own plan.

Years later, at the turn of the millennium, my son Marc was working at Atlantis Marina in Nassau, Bahamas, managing yachts for his successful company, Marine Professionals, Inc. (MPI).

One sunny day, as Marc was guiding a yacht into its slip, he noticed another vessel arriving—none other than the Continental Drifter II, Jimmy Buffett's 100-foot Cheoy Lee yacht. By sheer coincidence, their boats were docking side by side, setting the stage for an unforgettable moment.

Anticipation built as Marc waited for Jimmy to arrive. Soon enough, there he was—barefoot, wearing board shorts, and embodying the laid-back, island-living persona he was known for.

Marc seized the moment, introduced himself, and shared our connection.

What happened next?

That introduction would ultimately lead to me landing a full-time gig with Jimmy Buffett.

"Hi Jimmy, my name is Marc Curreri, I'm Capt. Lenny's son," my son introduced himself as Jimmy Buffett stepped barefoot onto the dock at Atlantis Marina in Nassau, Bahamas. Jimmy's face lit up with recognition. "How's Capt. Lenny doing these days?"

Marc responded, "He's doing great! Just flying around the world—but looking for the right job to finish his career."

Jimmy leaned in and, in a hushed tone, said, "I just bought a Falcon 50... *shhh*, no one knows yet."

Without missing a beat, Marc replied, "My dad is type-rated in that plane."

For those unfamiliar, flying larger jets requires special training and certifications—just because a pilot has a license doesn't mean they can fly any aircraft. The Falcon 50 required a specific type rating, something Jimmy's current captain didn't have.

Jimmy raised an eyebrow. "Oh, interesting, because we're looking for a captain with experience in the Falcon 50. Tell your dad that the plane will be managed by Shoreline Aviation in New Haven, Connecticut, and have him contact John Kelly."

Marc locked the name in his mind, repeating it internally as the conversation drifted into small talk about the best fish in the outer islands of the Bahamas.

The moment Marc had a chance, he called me—his excitement palpable. Halfway across the world in Ashgabat, Turkmenistan, while piloting a Challenger 601, I listened intently as he relayed the conversation.

Within minutes, I was on the phone with John Kelly. That call set off a chain of events that would shape the next chapter of my career.

In aviation, where every decision matters, this chance encounter with Jimmy Buffett was a perfect reminder of life's unpredictability—and the importance of seizing opportunities when they come your way. I soon joined Jimmy's team, embracing the unknown and trusting the journey ahead. As they say, "things happen for a reason."

THE NIGHT JIMMY BUFFETT BROKE THE "BAMBINO" CURSE

Fast forward to 2004—I was on tour with Jimmy Buffett, and he had planned something special for his Boston Parrot Heads.

That year, JB used Fenway Park as a venue to hype up his fan base in the area. Normally, he played two shows at Great Woods in Mansfield, Massachusetts, with a day off in between. That off day usually led to a clambake at our little beach house in Scituate, near that *"one particular harbor."*

On this particular night, my family and I had great seats—right behind John Henry, principal owner of the Red Sox. The Red Sox were facing the Yankees in the American League Championship Series. The stakes? The winner would go on to the World Series.

The problem? The Red Sox were down 3-0 in the seven-game series. A loss that night would eliminate them. Then came Jimmy Buffett's moment. On Friday night, September 10, 2004, he took center stage at Fenway Park. But before the music began, he orchestrated a surprise spectacle.

Wally Nickel, one of JB's production magicians, stepped onto the stage—dressed in a full Yankees pinstripe uniform, complete with Babe Ruth's #3 jersey. He had a Corona beer hanging out of his pocket, puffing on a cigar, looking every bit like the Ghost of the Bambino himself.

Jimmy grabbed a bat.

"Wally, let's get rid of the Babe's curse," Jimmy announced.

For 86 years, Red Sox fans had suffered under "The Curse of the Bambino." Ever since Babe Ruth was traded from the Red Sox to the Yankees after their 1918 World Series win, Boston had never won another championship. But that night, Jimmy made history.

Wally, dressed as Babe Ruth, lobbed a baseball toward JB. Crack!

Jimmy launched the ball into left field.

Crack!

He did it again.

Crack!

A third hit, deep into Fenway's historic outfield. Jimmy turned to the Red Sox faithful and said, *"That should do it. Go Red Sox!"*

What happened next?

The Red Sox won four straight games, beating the Yankees and pulling off one of the greatest comebacks in sports history. Then, they swept the St. Louis Cardinals in the World Series—finally breaking The Curse of the Bambino and becoming World Champions for the first time in 86 years. To this day, Boston fans will never forget what Jimmy Buffett did that night at Fenway Park. It's just another legendary tale about why people everywhere—especially in Boston—love and revere "Bubba" (aka Jimmy Buffett).

As I mentioned earlier, every year, between the two Great Woods shows in Mansfield, Massachusetts, we hosted Jimmy Buffett, the Coral Reefer Band, and the entire production crew at our little beach house in Scituate. It was a day to relax, recharge, and enjoy each other's company—a tradition that became one of the most cherished moments of the tour.

The crew would scour the beach for a lobster pot buoy that had washed ashore, and once found, everyone would sign it—a small but meaningful ritual that marked each year's gathering.

Our friends from Corona and other spirits companies made sure the drinks flowed, while the food was nothing short of a feast. Lobsters, clams, and home-cooked Italian meals were lovingly prepared by Elli and her mother, Connie—both incredible cooks who made sure no one left hungry. Side dishes covered every inch of the table, and there was always plenty to go around.

The guest list included a wide mix of the tour family—production crew, dancers, singers, the wardrobe team, Radio Margaritaville, and administrative staff. The Margaritaville security team ensured that everyone could let loose and enjoy the day, free from distractions. It was a rare moment of peace and privacy amid the chaos of a national tour.

(Little did we know that, 22 years later, just a few doors down from our beach house, an Oscar-nominated film—*American Fiction*—would be filmed, putting Sand Hills, Scituate, on the map!)

Many of the crew lived for this "day off"—a break from the constant movement of the tour, replaced with home-cooked meals, fresh Scituate seafood, and good old-fashioned "chowdah."

A huge thank you to Corona Reps, our sponsors, and the countless friends—many of whom I've lost track of over the years—who made these days as memorable as the shows themselves. These gatherings were more than just parties. They were a reminder that, beyond the music, beyond the travel, and beyond the stage lights, we were family.

HIDDEN RUNWAY 17L

Circa 2000-2010

In the summer of 1994, I was hired to help manage a Challenger CL-600 based in Munich and Berlin, Germany. This aircraft shared a hangar with an Antonov AN-2 at Lufthansa Technik Berlin Schoenfeld Airport (EDDB). The chief pilot was retiring, and they needed an immediate replacement for at least a year. After negotiations, I signed on for a three-year contract with the aircraft's owner—an incredibly interesting gentleman whose lifestyle and passions would take me on adventures I never expected.

The owner was a collector of castles throughout the European Union (EU) and had an obsession with antique clocks. To build his collection, he enlisted a Zurich-based clock expert, whom we simply referred to as "Clockman."

One of our more unusual missions involved retrieving a clock once owned by Napoleon Bonaparte. The clock had a massive marble base, gilded with gold detailing. Transporting it was no easy task. After carefully dismantling the base, we had to strategically secure it in the cabin of the Challenger—something that required some serious calculations and discussion. Eventually, we delivered it safely to his castle in Zeuten, near Berlin, where it was to remain permanently.

Another time, we flew him to Avignon, France, to view the world's first mechanical clock—a revolutionary invention that had replaced the sundial as the primary method of measuring time. This historic clock, housed in what was once the Papal residence (1309-1376), was loud and massive but proved that time could now be tracked without the sun.

By June 1998, I had taken on another fascinating opportunity. My dear friend Billy Witcher invited me to join him on a six-week trip to France with a Venezuelan family, covering the World Cup. Billy's wife, Rima, had just delivered their first child a few days before, so this was an eventful time for him. Also on board was Tom Kermode, who pulled double duty as Flight Mechanic and Flight Attendant on our Challenger CL 601-3A—one of two aircraft I had flown that had been blessed by Pope John.

Our journey began at Fort Lauderdale-Hollywood International Airport (FLL), with our first stop in Caracas, Venezuela. Shortly after departure, we encountered a minor glitch—a broken windshield heater relay. Thankfully, Tom quickly resolved the issue, allowing us to continue without delay.

Most of our time in France was spent north of Paris, based in a stunning hunting lodge at Le Bourget. The people we met there were equally fascinating—a couple who both flew FedEx routes between Paris and Moscow, along with other corporate aviation professionals who shared our passion for flying.

One Sunday, I asked the concierge if there was a Catholic church or chapel where I could attend Mass. She drew a map and gave me detailed directions. Since I knew the structure of a Catholic Mass, I wasn't concerned about understanding the French prayers—I could follow along without missing a beat.

The chapel was easy to find, and I arrived a little early as the parishioners began to gather. It was a beautiful and humbling experience.

As I stepped out of the chapel, I noticed an iron gate nearby, with what appeared to be a wooden propeller mounted at its center. Curious, I walked closer.

Just beyond the gate, I discovered three beautifully crafted crypts, each bearing inscriptions in French. Despite the language barrier, I could make out the birth and burial dates—and quickly realized these were the graves of three young pilots from different nations.

A French pilot.

A British pilot.

A German pilot.

None of them had lived past nineteen years old.

It became clear—they had engaged in a dogfight over this town during the Great War. Yet, rather than treating them as enemies, the local townspeople had honored them all with proper burials, side by side.

Even in war, there is humanity.

The Crypt for the British, French and German flyers from World War One.

18
FLIGHT 18R

While based in Germany from 1994 to 1997, our Challenger was hangared in Munich as well as Schoenfeld Airport (EDDB) in old East Berlin. Our aircraft's owner had a stunning castle on Lake Zeuthen, not far from EDDB, where we usually overnighted. Staying there was always an experience—being in the former East Berlin, the location carried a rich history, both before and after the Berlin Wall fell in 1989.

At EDDB, we quickly developed a strong friendship with Bernhard Conrad, the manager of the Lufthansa Technik facility. Bernhard went out of his way to help us hangar our Challenger, right next to Russia's biggest biplane—the Antonov AN-2. Thanks to Bernhard, I had the thrill of a lifetime, flying this legendary aircraft over Berlin at dusk.

Bernhard was also an airplane enthusiast, and during a trip to Venice, Florida, he purchased an Aeronca "Chief" tail-dragger. He had it shipped to Berlin and reassembled at EDDB, eager to fly it for his personal pleasure. However, he had never flown a tail-dragger before—and that's where I came in.

Since I was a U.S. CFI & A&I, I offered my services pro bono to train Bernhard, as a small token of appreciation for how well he treated us and our aircraft.

One of our more memorable

flights was a formation trip with three planes—a Super Cub, a Katana, and Bernhard's Chief—to Peenemünde, Germany. This was a historic site, known as the launch facility for the V-1 and V-2 rockets under Wernher von Braun during World War II.

While en route to Peenemünde, the Chief's window began to detach mid-flight, forcing Bernhard to make an emergency repair while airborne

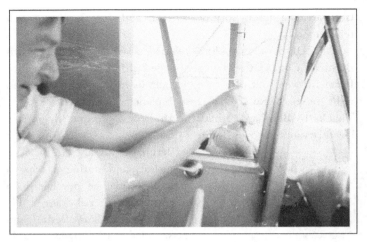

Bernhard making in-flight repairs on the way to Peenemünde in the Chief.

When we landed, I casually mentioned to the other pilots that I had actually "flown" with Wernher von Braun—a statement that stunned them into disbelief.

Back in Berlin, I continued flight training with Bernhard, taking him up in the Aeronca Chief whenever he needed instruction. Teaching him tail-dragger techniques, particularly the tricky ground taxi maneuvers using "heel brakes," was a workout for both of us. More than once, I found myself running alongside the plane on the Lufthansa Technik ramp at EDDB, shouting instructions as he learned how to turn in tight spots. It took some intense training, but we got the job done.

Bernhard also helped arrange some incredible flying experiences for me—including rides in the Antonov AN-2 and a JU-52 Lufthansa "Auntie JU." The JU-52 I flew had Pratt & Whitney Wasp engines, rather than the original Hispano-Suiza engines used in its early Spanish production models.

It was friendships like these, built through aviation, that turned every assignment into an unforgettable adventure.

19
FLIGHT 19L

Flying the Challenger always brought interesting experiences. My co-captain, Jamie, was invaluable—fluent in both German and Mandarin Chinese. Most of our flights took us to former Eastern Bloc cities, including Dresden, Leipzig, and Sofia, Bulgaria, as well as other airfields that presented unique challenges.

One particular trip to Sofia, Bulgaria, stands out. Our principal was scheduled to give a speech at the University of Sofia, but on the day of departure, we ran into a problem—the auxiliary power unit (APU) wouldn't start. Thankfully, we had built extra time into our schedule for unexpected hiccups.

The Challenger requires an air starter rather than an electric motor to start its engines. Luckily, Balkan Airlines operated Tupolev 134 and 154 aircraft, which used air starters—essentially copies of Rolls-Royce engines. I spoke with a young ground line manager who had the necessary ground equipment to fit a standard fitting. Using this, we successfully started the right-hand Lycoming ALF-502 engine, then cross-flowed air to start the other engine. Everything worked like clockwork—just as it had in the simulator.

Before we left, I thanked the young line manager and offered him a tip for his help, but he refused. Then, I noticed he was wearing a pair of Randall Engineering military-style sunglasses—

the same kind we used in the U.S. Navy. I mentioned that I was heading back to the States for the holidays and planned to visit Randall Engineering's headquarters near my home in Scituate, Massachusetts.

Later, when I met with Randall's VP of Marketing and shared the story of our technical troubles in Sofia, he had an idea. He suggested offering the young ground manager 100 pairs of sunglasses on consignment—an opportunity for him to become an agent for Randall in Bulgaria. The process was set in motion, and it turned into a win-win for both sides.

It's yet another example of how aviation brings people together, creating opportunities and unexpected connections across the world.

20
FLIGHT 20R

In 1997, our Challenger took us on a Far East trip through China, Vietnam, Oman, and India. The stop in Vietnam was particularly meaningful—it was my first time setting foot in a country I had only seen from a distance while serving aboard the aircraft carriers USS *Constellation* (CVA-64) and USS *Ranger* (CVA-61) some 30 years earlier.

During this trip, we parked next to a Gulfstream G-3 owned by Franklin Fidelity, a major financial institution. Onboard was Mark Mobius, a well-known investor, along with their pilot—a former Marine fighter pilot who had flown F-4 Phantoms out of Da Nang during the war. Mobius was eager to compare the two corporate aircraft models, though he seemed to prefer the comfort of the Challenger—though he wouldn't admit it outright.

Getting checked out in a MiG-21 CPT (Cockpit Procedures Trainer)

Attempting to enter the MIA/KIA office in Hanoi to inquire about one of my VA-146 squadron mates, Geoff Schmway, who was listed as MIA

Eating Vietnamese street food

Entering the Hanoi Hilton

One intriguing fact I learned during this visit was that the *Hanoi Hilton* actually had a women's quarters. Among its prisoners was a German nurse, Monika Schwinn, who had been captured on April 27, 1969. She remained incarcerated until January 27, 1973, when she was released as part of the Paris Peace Accords. She finally returned home to Germany on March 7, 1973.

21
FLIGHT 21L

Jimmy studying for his Falcon 900B checkout with friends—Doug Andrews, me, and Holly Shyduick, Chief Flight Attendant.

Randy, my "road wife," and me working in Hawaii!

My second tour with Randy for Jimmy Buffett began with a flight for Mrs. Buffett and some friends to a Texas resort near the Rio Grande—just four miles from the Mexican border. Before departing from Fort Worth Airport, I explained to Mrs. B that the weather at our destination was questionable, and since there was no instrument approach available, we might have to divert. Our backup plan was to land at an alternate airport about 80 miles from the resort and drive the rest of the way.

After some careful maneuvering—crossing briefly into Mexican airspace—we managed to land safely on the resort's private landing strip. As Mrs. Buffett stepped off the aircraft, I greeted her:

"Mrs. Buffett, I'm glad the weather cooperated so we could land at our final destination."

In her elegant South Carolinian drawl, she replied, "Lennie, you can call me Jane."

I thanked her but never took her up on the offer—out of deep respect for her and her family, she would always be "Mrs. Buffett" to me.

Early in the tour, Randy and I had a flight to Philadelphia

International Airport (KPHL), the closest airport to their Camden, NJ, venue. Our approach was set for Runway 26—a shorter, 5,000-foot runway that was conveniently near the FBO (Atlantic Aviation). As we configured the Falcon 50 for landing—deploying leading-edge slats and setting flaps to 20 degrees—we noticed the landing gear lowering unusually slowly. However, we still saw three green lights and heard no gear warning horn.

Then, just as we were about to turn final, the #1 hydraulic system failed.

The gauge read zero PSI, and the master caution panel lit up with a bright red *#1 HYD SYSTEM* warning. A quick glance at the checklist confirmed we had lost anti-skid and normal braking. With only the backup emergency braking system available, landing on the short Runway 26 was now out of the question.

We immediately requested a "side-step" maneuver to Runway 27R, a much longer 9,500-foot runway, which would allow for a controlled landing with minimal braking pressure to avoid blowing a tire. The landing itself was uneventful—just a slight turn on short final—and we taxied slowly to Atlantic Aviation.

As the passengers, including Jimmy and his band, gathered near the baggage compartment to retrieve their gear, we opened the baggage door and were met with a mess of red hydraulic fluid. It had leaked everywhere inside the equipment compartment, which housed the APU just behind the baggage area.

Jimmy, seeing the mess, asked, "What's that fluid?"

I explained that we had lost the #1 hydraulic system on final approach, forcing us to switch runways at the last minute and rely on emergency braking. He seemed unfazed, saying he hadn't noticed anything unusual about the landing—aside from the small course correction near the end.

"Well," I told him, "that's the whole point. It's supposed to feel normal."

Thankfully, Randy and I had just completed a DA-50 refresher course a week prior, which made all the difference. The culprit turned out to be a faulty hydraulic fuse, which had failed and blown a massive gap in the line, causing a total system loss.

Fortunately, the Falcon service center was just one town over in Wilmington, Delaware. By the next day, the system was fully repaired, and we were back on schedule—without missing a beat (pardon the pun).

One of my favorite stories took place in 2004, the day Jimmy Buffett officially earned his Pilot in Command (PIC)rating for the Falcon 50—a certification that also covered the Falcon 900, which he purchased shortly afterward.

At the time, Jimmy had accumulated about 519 hours as Second-in-Command (SIC) in the Dassault Falcon 50 (DA-50). He had worked tirelessly through training sessions, both in the aircraft and in ground school, where we practiced approaches and maneuvers in the Miami-Dade Collier Airport (KTNT)—a remote airfield in the middle of the Florida Everglades.

Originally built as a dedicated training field for airlines like Eastern, National, and Pan Am, KTNT was designed to maximize cost and time efficiency for airline training. However, with the advent of Level D flight simulators, pilots no longer needed to fly actual aircraft to maintain currency. As a result, the airfield became a quieter training ground—perfect for corporate aviation, where pilots could train without worrying about traffic congestion or close mid-air encounters.

By then, Jimmy was no stranger to jet aircraft—he already held a CE500 jet rating and an HU-16 Albatross type rating, so he was familiar with FAA performance and handling requirements. For his Falcon 50 PIC check ride, I arranged for Captain Mark Potter, an FAA Designated Pilot Examiner, to oversee the flight. I would sit in the right seat to monitor the maneuvers, while Captain Potter handled the oral and familiarization portion of the exam.

That day, Captain Potter had a guest in town—a Bacardi Rum executive—who asked if he could sit in the cabin and observe the check ride. Knowing that Jimmy could go either way on this, I asked him for approval. True to his laid-back and generous nature, Jimmy simply said:

"Sure, as long as he stays in the main cabin."

Just over 45 minutes later, after flawlessly executing every maneuver and approach we had practiced, we taxied back to the Jet Aviation ramp at PBI (Palm Beach International Airport).

Captain Potter stepped up to the cockpit, shook Jimmy's hand, and said, "Congratulations, Captain Buffett! You nailed it." He then signed him off as a DA-50/900 Captain.

Jimmy was a very happy new Falcon 50 captain, later becoming Managing Director and Chief Pilot for Air Margaritaville—proving himself not only as an exceptional jet pilot, but also a masterful seaplane aviator.

A very happy Captain Jimmy Buffett, earning his Pilot-in-Command privileges in the Falcon 50 and 900 in 2004.

I think Doug has the right idea! "Going to see Jimmy. Back Maybe Never!"

22

HIDDEN RUNWAY 22R

Before one of our early European trips, I received an email from a Mr. Joe Merchant. He ran a bar at Biggin Hill Airport in London and invited Randy and me to join him for a beer at his pub, *The Pilot's Pals*. Of all the airport bars in the world, Biggin Hill's was known for its lively characters, and Joe was certainly one of them. He was convinced that *Where Is Joe Merchant?*, Jimmy Buffett's No. 1 *New York Times* bestseller, was about him.

Joe had spent time in Africa on a photo shoot featuring antique airplanes and female models for his annual Biggin Hill calendar, a favorite holiday gift among the local aviation crowd. That particular year, he had also been promoting his bar with bumper stickers that read: *"Where is Joe Merchant?"* and *"Joe Merchant, phone home."* According to Joe, these stickers had been plastered all over bars in Africa, and he firmly believed that Jimmy must have seen them and gotten the idea for the book's title.

Curiosity got the best of us. Was Joe Merchant really the inspiration for *Where Is Joe Merchant?* Had Jimmy unknowingly taken the title from this mysterious Biggin Hill figure? Randy and I decided to find out, making a quick stop at Biggin Hill to meet the man himself.

Joe was in fine form that night, doing what he did best—

entertaining two pilots with legendary tales over pints of beer. We humored him, but as the night went on, he became increasingly adamant that he was *the* Joe Merchant. At one point, he even pulled out a book cover that looked different from Jimmy's official version. This oddity gave us pause, but we decided not to challenge his claim too directly. Instead, we simply enjoyed the evening, laughed along, and let the mystery remain unsolved.

As the night wrapped up, Joe graciously arranged for a *Black Taxi* to take us back to our hotel. We left *Pilot's Pals* with new friends, but no clearer answer as to whether this Joe Merchant had anything to do with Jimmy's book. Some wondered whether Joe Merchant of Biggin Hill ever truly existed, and Randy later commented that although Jimmy had never met him, the tale of our boss seeing those stickers in African bars continued to follow us in our travels. Since Jimmy had written the book years earlier, we never brought the story up to him—and, as far as we know, Joe Merchant eventually moved to Spain, where he's now enjoying retirement on a British pension.

One thing's for sure: Joe Merchant firmly *believed* Jimmy's book was about him, and to this day, his legend lives on among the patrons of *Pilot's Pals*.

Most people don't realize that Jimmy Buffett held a rare literary distinction. At the time, he was one of only six authors to have a No. 1 bestseller on the *New York Times* list in both fiction and nonfiction—a club that included his literary hero, Ernest Hemingway.

After our stop in London, we continued our travels through Fez, Marrakech, and Casablanca, Morocco; Luxor, Egypt; Kilimanjaro, Tanzania; Zanzibar; Johannesburg, South Africa; São Tomé, Cape Verde; Barbados; and finally home to West Palm Beach, Florida.

23
FLIGHT 23L

Randy and me in our Moroccan "Uniform of the Day"

While in Morocco, we visited Marrakech, Casablanca, and Fez. Near the end of our stay, I received a call from Jimmy asking if I could land at an old military base in the Sahara Desert—the planned endpoint of his family's camel caravan.

He gave me the basic airfield information and then ended the conversation with, "Please say hi to Bob."

I turned to Randy. *"Do you know who Bob is?"*

Randy had no clue. My next call was to Mike Ramos back in the States to see if he could track down this "Bob." I couldn't reach him, but I vaguely remembered hearing that Robert Redford (aka Bob) was in Morocco filming a new movie.

After a few calls, I finally got through to the concierge at the Hyatt Hotel in Casablanca, who confirmed that Redford had already left town—mission complete.

Capt. Buffett and Leslie—safely navigating our flight over Morocco in fez attire!

As for landing at a remote, abandoned airfield in the Sahara, the Moroccan FAA was not having it. They made it clear: No EU charter certificate, no landing. Processing the paperwork would take at least a week—not to mention the insurance nightmare of getting approval for such an operation.

The next morning, I called JB with the update. I told him that *Bob* had already left Morocco, and that getting permission to land at the desert airstrip was a definite no-go.

Jimmy took it in stride, but he was preoccupied with something else. "I'm sitting on a camel right now, wearing a turban just like the Moroccan Berbers or Bedouins. If someone takes a picture of me, this could be a great album cover for my next record."

At the time, this was early 2001—before 9/11. He was considering using the image for what would become The Far Side of the World.

However, after September 11, 2001, Jimmy reconsidered. Any Arab-themed imagery, including him on a camel, suddenly felt like a bad idea. The album still kept its name, but the concept shifted.

Still, JB was kind enough to give Randy, Billy Schmidt, and me a shoutout in the "Special Thanks" section of the album credits—along with many others who had been part of the journey.

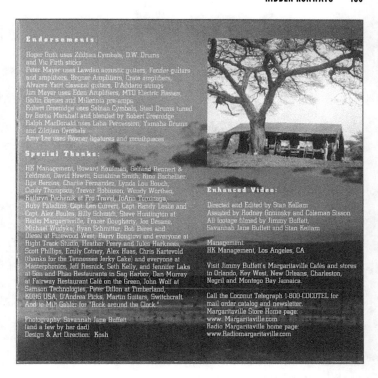

While in Luxor, Egypt, Randy and I were invited by JB to join him, his son Cameron, and a staff member on a hot air balloon ride over the *Valley of the Kings* in a 13-person basket. The evening before, JB called and asked if I could conduct a personal safety audit of the balloon company. I tracked down a phone number for the company and called. A Brit answered, claiming to be the owner of the operation. He assured me that Mohammed, our assigned pilot, was the best balloon pilot they had and that we would be safe and enjoy the ride

At 0530 the next morning, we were asked to assemble on the west side of the Nile, where a boat—something straight out of *The African Queen*—would ferry us to the balloon ascension area. Right on cue, Randy and I arrived at the dock, where Mohammed greeted us and delivered an impressive safety briefing on all possible *what-if* scenario

As we approached the arrival dock, I happened to glance off to the right side of our water taxi—and that's when I saw it. Moored nearby was an incredibly beautiful Egyptian boat—not a traditional *Felucca*-style vessel, but one straight out of an old *National Geographic* spread. Painted on the bow in bold letters was: "Bob Marley."

I couldn't believe my eyes.

After our incredible balloon ride—and a celebratory dance by Mohammed's ground crew—I walked over to JB and asked, "Did you see that boat with Bob Marley's name on it?"

He hadn't. But as soon as I told him, he immediately had an idea.

"I need you to help me get some video of me sailing that thing for the Jumbotrons on tour."

Sure enough, after our successful (and safe) balloon ride, JB headed straight for the shoreline, determined to track down the *Bob Marley* boat and make his wish come true. You never know what to expect on a Jimmy Buffett adventure!

Jimmy and Randy flying over the Valley of the Kings

Departing Luxor, we followed the eastern coast of the Nile and headed for Kilimanjaro. The weather was terrible—we couldn't even see the top of Kilimanjaro, and the instrument approach was a bit tricky. Still, we arrived safely and without incident.

A bush caravan pulled up next to us almost immediately, ensuring an efficient transfer of passengers and baggage. After watching the Buffetts disappear into the bush in their caravan, Randy and I cranked up the Falcon 50 and set course for Lanseria, South Africa (RSA), near Johannesburg. That's where we planned to hangar the plane for a couple of weeks over the Christmas holiday.

Somewhere along the way, we suddenly lost all GPS navigation capability. That was highly unusual. Fortunately, we had backup systems—IRS, VOR, and NDB navigation—so we continued without major issues. Later, we learned that someone was electronically jamming the satellite signals—most likely the Russians!

After a two-week break, we returned to Johannesburg from Atlanta on a South African Airways Boeing 747, a brutal 18½-hour flight. But we were ready to resume the adventure.

We headed back up the east coast of Africa, stopping at Johannesburg's OR Tambo Airport (formerly Jan Smuts International) before continuing to Zanzibar, Tanzania. The schedule was constantly changing, depending on what new experiences JB and his family wanted to explore. After Jo'burg, JB mentioned an intriguing next stop—São Tomé, a small nation on the west coast of Africa that I had never even heard of until he brought it up.

It wasn't on any list of "terrorist nations," but it definitely wasn't a typical travel destination. I reached out to my Yellow Team contacts at Universal Weather and Aviation Inc., and our trusted aircraft handlers confirmed it was safe. With that reassurance, we planned the next leg of our African journey.

As we approached São Tomé, the airwaves were eerily quiet—not unusual for this part of the world. But what *was* unusual was the São Tomé control tower's next transmission:

"There are animals on the runway."

Specifically, water buffalo had wandered onto the landing zone. We asked if they could be moved before landing, and the tower responded by sending out a "Follow Me" vehicle to clear them. We slowed to minimum approach speed and carefully watched the situation unfold.

JB, as the flying pilot, handled it with complete professionalism. Once we were sure the runway was clear, he executed a smooth landing, aligning perfectly—sans any stray water buffalo in our path.

The same "Follow Me" vehicle guided us to the overnight parking area, where we spotted two Russian-registered aircraft:

- A Grumman G-159
- A Yakovlev Yak-30

We checked in with our handler, confirming that our safety status hadn't changed. They assured us that we were good for an overnight stay, so we secured N502JB and headed to the hotel.

Later that night, JB called and said, "Let's leave early in the morning for Cape Verde. Plan for an overnight." Another adventure was on the horizon.

We blasted out of São Tomé around 08:30 AM, starting a 4½-hour flight to Cape Verde. As we descended, the landscape surrounding the airport looked completely alien—barren, rocky, and otherworldly.

Right as we touched down, JB's voice came through the headset:

"Are we on the moon?"

Our stay in Cape Verde remained "open-ended," with Randy and me on standby status for further instructions. Early that evening, we finally received our marching orders—next stop: Barbados, approximately 2,300 nautical miles west of Cape Verde.

To put it in perspective, the distance was about the same as flying from San Francisco to Hawaii. Our route would take us along the equator, right through the notorious "doldrums"—a region of equatorial calms known for very light upper-level and surface winds.

When I briefed Jimmy on the flight plan, he responded in the way only a Son of a Son of a Sailor would—completely confident in the mission ahead. He understood the Falcon 50's capabilities, as well as our planned divert option: Ascension Island, located about eight degrees south of the equator—roughly midway between Africa (1,600 km away) and Barbados (2,300 km away).

Normally, landing on Ascension Island required prior permission, since it was a joint RAF (Royal Air Force) and USAF base. So, we alerted our Universal Aviation Yellow Team to advise

ATC and airport personnel of our flight plan, just in case we needed to divert.

Despite encountering stronger-than-expected doldrum winds, we arrived in Barbados within 15 minutes of our planned flight time—a testament to our careful planning and the reliability of the Falcon 50. And unlike our previous stop, there were no tower advisories about animals on the runway—what a relief!

Our stay in Barbados was brief, and the next day we continued on to West Palm Beach, bringing an exciting and unforgettable family adventure across the Dark Continent to a close.

The Captain and the Kid (Cameron)))

*Remembering Larry "Groovy" Gray, President of "Air Mango"
and dear friend of the Buffett family.*

24

FLIGHT 24R

After a break from flying for tour activities, our next journey would take us to Ecuador and the Galápagos Islands. Our first stop was Quito, Ecuador's capital, where we planned to park N502JB at a friend's hangar. However, before we could do that, we were greeted by an unexpected sight at the end of Quito's 10,000-foot runway.

"Quito Surprise"

Since the Galápagos Islands had no jet fuel, we based our plane out of Guayaquil, Ecuador, an excellent sea-level airport that allowed for easy round-trip flights to the Galápagos without needing to refuel there.

At the end of this adventure, I reminded JB that we had to depart from the Ecuadorian mainland to comply with U.S. and Ecuadorian customs and immigration regulations. But in classic JB fashion, he had another idea.

He told me he had a legal way for us to fly directly from the Galápagos to West Palm Beach, bypassing the Ecuadorian mainland. The direct route was 1,725 nautical miles—within our Falcon 50's capabilities with proper fuel management and a planned divert option if needed. Normally, this kind of direct international flight would be impossible without official authorization.

However, Jimmy had connections. He knew a VIP in the Ecuadorian government who secured a special letter of approval allowing us to take off directly from the Galápagos. After confirming everything with U.S. Immigration and Border Control, we were cleared for departure. The flight went smoothly, and thanks to JB's Ecuadorian friends, we pulled off yet another Air Margaritaville miracle.

With that adventure behind us, we set off for another family trip—this time to Machu Picchu, Peru. Both Machu Picchu and

Cusco sit at over 10,000 feet MSL, which meant we had to modify our Falcon 50's pressurization system. A simple Service Bulletin update allowed our cabin pressurization to operate up to 15,000 feet, ensuring a comfortable flight at high altitudes.

When the day arrived, we flew to Lima, Peru, where we picked up a Peruvian FAA inspector who would officially sign us off for flying into Cusco. Sitting in the jump seat between Randy and me, he briefed us on the Air Peru Escape Route—a specific procedure for handling engine failure immediately after takeoff from Cusco's Teniente A. Velasco Astete International Airport (SPZO), which sits at 10,860 feet MSL.

Upon approach to Runway 28 at Cusco, we descended to 12,700 feet MSL—the Minimum Descent Altitude (MDA). However, we were still in the clouds. I told the inspector we were executing a missed approach, but he insisted we continue another 100 feet lower.

I exchanged a glance with Randy. We agreed to give it a few more seconds—but before we reached 12,600 feet, the runway came into view. I immediately requested a visual approach and received clearance to land.

After a smooth touchdown, our passengers cleared customs with assistance from Universal Weather & Aviation's ground handlers. The Peruvian FAA inspector debriefed us, acknowledging our professionalism and strict adherence to safety protocols. He handed us an official letter of approval, confirming we were now "certified" to fly this route.

With N502JB secured at the airport, we headed to our hotel in Cusco—The Monasterio, a former 16th-century monastery that had been converted into an Inca-style luxury hotel.

Checking in, I noticed an interesting room service request option: "More O_2". Since Cusco sits at nearly 11,000 feet MSL, some guests experienced altitude sickness. For $25 per night, you could have extra oxygen pumped into your room. I immediately checked the box, recalling how out of breath I had been landing in La Paz, Bolivia years ago—a 13,000-foot MSL airport with a 13,000-foot runway. That time, I had nearly passed out climbing the tower stairs to file a flight plan!

The Monasterio stay was unique—from the traditional Inca dinner featuring Alpaca steak, to the waitstaff dressed in Inca attire. But one thing started to get on our nerves—the constant background music. It had apparently been playing nonstop since the friars first occupied the monastery in the 1600s!

Despite the monotonous music, the extra O_2 helped me sleep, making the $25 upgrade well worth it.

On the morning of our departure, we made an early trip to the airport to burn off 1,500 pounds of fuel before takeoff. This was a precautionary measure to comply with the Air Peru Escape Route weight restrictions—just in case we had an engine failure on takeoff.

With plenty of fuel for our short flight to Lima, we made a tech stop before heading back to West Palm Beach.

Back home, Randy and I waited with bated breath for our next assignment—beyond our usual tour-related flights.

And the winner was...?

25
FLIGHT 25L

It was during the political season of 2000, and Jimmy had offered his support to Al Gore in his campaign for U.S. President. His Falcon 50 would serve as his transport to various campaign rallies where he would serenade the crowds before Gore took the stage.

One particular stop took us to Tampa, Florida, where we were scheduled to meet up with Air Force Two (AF2) at Tampa International Airport (TPA) before heading to a rally. Jimmy's N502JB was supposed to park nose-to-nose with AF2—a surreal sight for any pilot.

Jimmy's N502JB nose-to-nose with Air Force Two during the 2000 Al Gore presidential campaign in Cincinnati, Ohio.

As we approached TPA, we tuned into the Airport Terminal Information System (ATIS) and heard an unexpected issue—Runway 36R was closed. This was problematic because that's where Air Force Two was parked for our rendezvous with Gore and his team.

Jimmy, sitting in the jump seat, was growing impatient. We were already running behind schedule, and in classic JB fashion, he leaned forward and said:

"Tell the tower I'm on board and insist on using Runway 36R!"

The problem? Runway 36R (now designated 01R) had strict noise abatement procedures.

Before I could respond, my trusty road wife Randy, a longtime friend of JB, turned to him and said:

"Jimmy, I don't think that's a good idea."

JB looked at him. "Why not?"

Randy grinned and said:

"If, by chance, the ATC tower controller is a REPUBLICAN, we may not get permission to land on our favored runway—especially since it's a noise abatement corridor."

Jimmy paused. "You got a point."

I carefully picked up the mic and worded our request strategically—asking if we could land on Runway 36R to minimize taxi time while assuring them we'd follow strict noise abatement procedures. The controller granted our request—as long as we didn't exceed the Effective Perceived Noise Levels (EPnda) limits.

We landed smoothly and quietly, but upon arrival, we got some bad news—Al Gore had already left for the rally.

We relayed this to JB, but he simply smiled and said:

"I don't think the crowd is waiting for him to speak. Maybe they know I'm coming along and won't mind the delay—because I'll be serenading them."

Most likely true.

Flying with Senator Bob Graham

At the rally, I was approached with a new mission: I was asked to pick up former Florida Governor and U.S. Senator Bob

Graham in our Amphibian Caravan and fly him wherever he needed to go.

As soon as the senator boarded, he turned to me and said:

"Captain, I'm breaking two of my cardinal rules by flying with you today."

I asked what they were.

"First, I swore I would never fly in a single-engine turboprop aircraft."

"And the second?" I asked.

"I promised myself I'd never fly without at least two pilots onboard. But I'm breaking both rules because JB says you're not only 'OKAY' to fly with, but that he lets his own family fly with you—so that's good enough for me."

I thanked him for the vote of confidence, and we took off for Miami Executive Airport (KTMB, formerly Tamiami Airport).

During the flight, we had an unexpectedly bipartisan, friendly conversation. Senator Graham shared stories about his dairy farms, explaining the art of milking cows—which I assured him I'd follow precisely *if* I ever found myself in that situation.

He also told me about his "Save the Manatee" foundation, which he co-founded with Jimmy. By the time we landed, I had learned more about manatees than I ever thought I would—and developed a newfound respect for the cause.

Soon, another trip was in the works—this time, to Argentina. Another unforgettable adventure awaited.

26
FLIGHT 26R

We departed Palm Beach International (PBI) with a planned technical (fuel) stop in Lima, Peru, before continuing to Buenos Aires, Argentina. Our destination was Aeroparque Jorge Newbery (AEP)—the city's downtown airport, similar to LaGuardia (LGA) in New York.

Since some Argentinian ATC towers lacked English-speaking staff, we brought along a FlightSafety pilot named Glen, a Spanish speaker, to assist with communications.

At the time of our departure, Argentina was experiencing civil unrest, with expected demonstrations and disruptions. We checked with our contacts at Universal Weather and Aviation, as well as State Department and government sources, all of whom assured us it was safe to proceed—but advised caution.

After discussing the situation with JB, he agreed to move forward with the trip.

Following a brief stay in Buenos Aires, we began planning visits to Bariloche, El Calafate, and Mendoza—with Bariloche being the first stop.

Bariloche felt like a little piece of Switzerland—a stunning town with mountain views, alpine architecture, and pristine lakes. While staying at our hotel, we ran into the crew of Ted Turner's Challenger jet, who were also in town.

As pilots do, we had some "hangar talk"—trading stories

about flying, international operations, and their trip itinerary. They were only there for one night before heading back to Atlanta (ATL). Turner himself was checking in on his bison cattle farms, which supplied meat for his Bison Steak restaurant chain.

Our next stop was El Calafate, famous for its majestic icebergs.

On our first night there, JB called me with a new idea: "Len, let's take a trip to the end of the world!"

I knew we were in South America, but I wasn't exactly sure what he meant.

He clarified:

"I'm talking about Ushuaia, on the island of Tierra del Fuego."

Ushuaia sits at 54° South Latitude—roughly 2,300 miles from Antarctica—making it the southernmost city and airport on the planet. It is also the closest departure point for cruise ships heading to Antarctica.

We contacted Argentinian ATC to discuss a VFR/IFR flight plan that would allow our passengers the best possible viewing and video opportunities.

After takeoff from El Calafate, we found a clear area where we could safely remain VFR, capturing incredible views of the blue icebergs.

It was a busy flight, balancing navigation, cloud clearance, and safety maneuvers, while also ensuring our passengers had a breathtaking experience.

As we approached Ushuaia, we passed by the Faro Les Eclaireurs lighthouse (nicknamed "The Scouts"), a famous landmark just outside the city's harbor. The sight of the lighthouse signaled our final approach to the southernmost airport in the world.

Jimmy flying his Falcon 50 during our trip to the "End of the World" ahead!

Another unforgettable flight in the Air Margaritaville logbook!

After landing, JB and his guests went downtown for lunch, saying they'd be back in about an hour and a half. Glen Yazercheck and I took advantage of the time and found a nearby restaurant. Inside, we noticed a massive photograph of a Tower Air Boeing 747 landing at Ushuaia Airport. Curious, we asked about the image and learned that during the Falklands War, Tower Air played a key role in supplying Ushuaia with goods while also supporting Antarctic expeditions by delivering provisions to research teams stationed there.

Almost three hours passed before JB and his guests returned. He had thoroughly enjoyed his meal, which included tasting some of Argentina's famous Malbec grapes. Feeling relaxed, he suggested Glen and I fly back to El Calafate. I asked if he wanted to be notified when we passed over Ted Turner's bison ranch—he declined.

Back in El Calafate, we prepared for our return to Buenos Aires, or so we thought. Before JB left the airport, he asked if there was any chance we could land at the Argentinian Navy Base at Punta Indio. I told him I'd check into it. That evening, I reached out to our contacts at Universal Weather and Aviation, as well as the base authorities. After some coordination, I was able to speak directly with the Skipper of the base, and he arranged for a landing permit.

There was one issue—insurance. While we had secured coverage for previous military base landings during JB's USO trips to Guantanamo Bay, Cuba, Punta Indio was not a U.S. base. After some negotiations, we obtained the necessary approval and finalized our flight plan.

Upon landing at Punta Indio, I met with the base's commanding officer, and we discovered an unexpected connection. The Skipper had completed his carrier qualifications in an Argentinian Douglas A-4B "Scooter" (also known as an A-4AR "Fighting Hawk") aboard the USS *Constellation* (CVA-64)—the same aircraft carrier I had served on during my first combat cruise to Point Yankee in the Tonkin Gulf. We immediately hit it off, sharing stories about carrier landings and military aviation.

As a parting gift, the Skipper gave me an A-4B "Fuerza Aerea Argentina" ashtray as a keepsake, which I still have. JB thoroughly enjoyed the visit and was grateful to reconnect with his friends at the base. After our short stay, we returned to Buenos Aires and began planning our flight home.

For our return to PBI, we scheduled a stop at a civil-military airport near Lima, Peru, with a landing time of approximately 4:30 AM local. This flight taught me an invaluable lesson—one that could have led to a major issue had I not thoroughly reviewed all thirty pages of NOTAMs. Even with years of experience flying international routes, I was reminded how critical it is to carefully analyze every detail of a flight plan to ensure the safety of the crew and passengers.

While reviewing the 30 pages of NOTAMs, I noticed a crucial detail on page 29—our planned tech stop airport had its only runway (05/23) listed as being in "survey mode" between 02:30 and 06:30 AM. I wasn't sure if that meant the runway was closed or if it would be available for us upon arrival. With only four hours before departure, I contacted our Yellow Team at Universal Weather (UV-Air) to get clarification. An hour passed with no response. When UV-Air finally got back to me, they said the Peruvian authorities couldn't provide a clear answer. That was enough for me to make the call. I instructed UV-Air to cancel our planned stop and switch to Lima (SPIM), a 24-hour airport we were familiar with.

After we safely arrived back at PBI, the Peruvian authorities finally responded, confirming that the airport would have been closed during our scheduled arrival time. That could have been a disaster if we hadn't caught it in time. A big lesson learned—always read all NOTAMs thoroughly and never assume. If something is unclear, it's always safer to adjust plans than to take unnecessary risks. Thankfully, UV-Air was with us all the way, ensuring our flight was safe and efficient.

One thing that stood out about Argentina was its Malbec wine. It was everywhere—plentiful, affordable, and outstanding. I made sure to bring back a case or two to enjoy later.

One of the most exciting things Jimmy got to do was fly the Sikorsky S-38, the rare amphibian aircraft featured in *The Aviator* (2004), where Leonardo DiCaprio played Howard Hughes. JB had expressed interest in flying one of these classic birds, so I did some digging and found Tom Schrade, the owner of one of only two flying S-38s in the world. Tom generously offered JB—and me—the chance to take the controls and experience what it was like to fly this 1927-era beauty

Tom Schrade in his plane

Another unique adventure came when JB and Cameron were invited to join a U.S. Coast Guard midshipman cruise aboard the Barque Eagle, a legendary tall ship used for training. JB wanted to be dropped off in Salem, MA Harbor, where the Eagle was anchored, and then picked up at the end of the cruise in Provincetown Harbor for the return trip to East Hampton.

To make this work, I had to get clearance from both the Salem and Provincetown Harbor Masters for amphibious landings. After a few meetings and discussions, we got the approvals.

During the cruise, from August 13–15, 2002, JB and Cameron climbed to the highest sail points, the Royal Arms, and took in the breathtaking views. JB also captured footage for use on Jumbotron videos at his shows, adding another piece of adventure to his on-stage storytelling.

From flying vintage amphibians to sailing aboard a tall ship, Jimmy Buffett always found a way to turn every trip into an adventure.

27
FLIGHT 27L

Buffett family arriving at Deauville-Normandie Airport as invited guests for the 60th anniversary of D-Day, June 6, 2004. Cameo appearance by staff member Darin Hinson.

During the summer of 2004, JB and his family were invited to attend the 60th anniversary of D-Day in Normandy, France. The plan was to depart from Francis S. Gabreski Airport (KFOK) on Long Island, NY, which had a long enough runway for us to fly nonstop to Deauville-Normandie Airport (LFRG), France.

As we were preparing for departure, we noticed an amber "Fuel Computer" light illuminated on the Master Caution panel after starting engine #2. The problem? A failed Manual Mode computer, meaning we couldn't safely take off until it was repaired.

Luckily, we were close to a Garrett Engine service center, and we obtained written ferry flight permission for a five-minute flight to Islip Airport (KISP) with engine #2 in manual mode. The mechanics made a quick fix and calibration, and before long, we were back on course, heading across the Atlantic to Normandy with minimal inconvenience to our passengers.

Like an old instructor once told me: "Expect the unexpected." This time, we were fortunate that the issue happened where it did and not midway over the ocean.

The transatlantic flight was uneventful, and our passengers arrived at Deauville-Normandie Airport as scheduled. Randy and I then repositioned N502JB to Le Bourget Airport (LFPB) in Paris, where we planned to leave the aircraft while we took part in the historic celebrations.

The next day, we rented a car and made our way to Normandy, eager to take part in the commemorations of the greatest seaborne invasion in history.

We visited the D-Day landing beaches—Utah, Gold, Omaha, Juno, and Sword—as well as several historical displays that detailed the events of June 6, 1944, and the hard-fought battles that followed. Standing on those beaches, it was hard to fathom the sheer magnitude of what had happened there. The courage, sacrifice, and resilience of those who fought were beyond words.

Me and Randy at the D-Day Museum, checking out THE JEEP!!

While passing by a British military cemetery, I approached a decorated British veteran to personally express my gratitude. Shaking his hand, I said:

"You and your British comrades are to be commended for your bravery. It was a lousy war, and you and your mates were truly part of the Greatest Generation."

The soldier looked at me and asked, "Were you in a war?"

I hesitated for a moment and answered, "It was more of a conflict—the Vietnam conflict, 1964–1967."

He looked me in the eye and said, "You must have had a rough time and situation."

I shook my head. "No, sir. I was stationed on a 'Bird Farm'— two different U.S. aircraft carriers, the *Constellation* and *Ranger*— primarily on the flight deck as an ordnance and avionics officer. I had clean sheets on my bed every night, and I wasn't personally shot at like my squadron mates who flew A-4Cs. They were the ones launched off the deck, hoping to return safely."

The veteran nodded, understanding the distinction, but still with the deep respect of someone who knew the cost of war. Randy and I shook his hand one more time before continuing our journey to visit as many sites as possible.

Me at the British cemetery after shaking hands with some brave British vets.

Being part of the D-Day 60th anniversary events was one of the most humbling and memorable experiences of my flying career.

28
FLIGHT 28R

During my time with "Sails in Concert," one of the most memorable encounters I had was with "Uncle" Walter Cronkite. One of our missions was to pick up JB and Mr. Cronkite at Napa Valley Airport and transport them across the country to East Hampton Airport (HTO) and Martha's Vineyard Airport (MVY), Walter's final stop.

Both Walter and JB had just attended the Bohemian Grove encampment, a highly exclusive private gentlemen's club for the rich and powerful. The club was known for its strict membership policies, and even JB had to buy a sport jacket just to interview for membership—a rare sight for him. It reminded me of when Warren Buffett dressed JB properly for the introduction of the Cheeseburger in Paradise restaurant chain in Omaha, Nebraska.

The weather for the trip was far from ideal. Thunderstorms and heavy winds were forecasted at both destinations. Before takeoff, I advised both JB and Walter that if conditions did not improve, we might have to drop JB off at Suffolk County Airport (FOK) and figure out Walter's arrival plan later.

The cross-country flight itself was smooth, but as we neared East Hampton, the weather had not improved. We diverted to FOK and arranged for transportation to take JB home to Sag Harbor. After refueling and ensuring Walter was comfortable, we continued further east to Martha's Vineyard.

The flight into MVY was bumpy, to say the least. Strong winds and thick cloud cover made for a challenging approach, but Walter remained his usual calm and collected self. As we helped him off the plane, he turned to Randy and me and said:

"Captain, there sure was a lot of clouds on this flight!"

That was an understatement.

As he disembarked, he thanked us for a safe flight and insisted on introducing us to his wife and daughter, who had just arrived in their Texas-registered Mercedes. It was just another example of JB's generosity—offering Walter a safe, comfortable ride home despite the challenging weather conditions.

A few days later, Walter's secretary called to thank us again for the safe flight. Then, two days after that, we received an autographed photo of Walter with a gold-inlaid inscription that read:

"To Len Curreri (and congratulations to Randy too), The best pilots in all of Margaritaville! Your Friend, Walter Cronkite."

What an honor.

In the years that followed, before Walter's passing, JB made a point of flying into New York City on our Caravan on floats, landing at the 23rd Street Seaplane Base to personally serenade Walter at his residence. Wearing one of his favorite Hawaiian shirts, JB would play Walter's favorite Margaritaville tunes on his ukulele, making for a truly special sendoff for one of the most respected journalists in history.

29
FLIGHT 29L

After retiring from Sails in Concert and my time as Jimmy Buffett's pilot, I was fortunate to spend more time with my wife and our kids, Cristina and Marc, watching them both become successful entrepreneurs.

Marc built a marine business empire, owning four companies:
- MPI – Marine Professionals
- Scituate Boat Works
- Monahan's Marine Supply
- Dockmate US

Cristina, meanwhile, founded the Scituate Salt Cave in our hometown.

Beyond our kids' success, retirement also allowed us to spend more time with our grandkids—Ella, Emily, Jackson, and Jake—watching them grow into their own special personalities, giving us even more to love and cherish.

Though I had stepped away from the Parrot Head adventures, I wasn't quite ready to hang up my wings. I moved into contract pilot work, leveraging an extensive rolodex of flight operations contacts from my years of flying the Falcon 50 and 900.

One of my best flying gigs came from a referral by a former Chief Pilot, leading to regular flights for a company that employed some of the most professional and talented pilots I had ever worked with. I had the pleasure of flying with Carlo, Willy, Andrea, Brenno, Alois, Edigio, and Giorgio—a group of top-notch aviators who also happened to be incredible company. When we weren't in the air, we were sharing great meals and swapping stories in some of the best restaurants around the world.

My international flying expanded, including two of my longest nonstop flights ever:

- Bozeman, Montana (KBZN) to London, UK (EGKB)
- Saint Maarten (TNCM) to Lugano, Switzerland (LSZA)

Both legs were over 4,000 NM and more than nine hours in the air. Special thanks to "Chocolate Willy" for that opportunity!

Beyond flying, I also served as their FAR 61.58 check airman, providing training and proficiency checks for their pilots. Despite the title, I wasn't training aliens from another planet— just foreign pilots operating under U.S. FAA standards. The company's fleet included a Falcon 900EX and a Falcon 100, plus a mix of general aviation single and twin-engine aircraft, keeping things interesting and challenging.

This contract work lasted for several years, always bringing something new and exciting to the table.

One particularly memorable trip took me to Tours, France, near the owner's residence. He highly recommended taking the back roads to Amboise, home to Château du Clos Lucé—the final residence of Leonardo da Vinci.

During the Renaissance period (1400–1600 AD), King Francis I of France invited Leonardo to live in Amboise as a sign of their friendship. From 1516 to 1519, Leonardo called Château du Clos Lucé home.

Walking through the château was like stepping back in time. It housed models of Leonardo's inventions, including his "Aero Screw"—a precursor to the modern helicopter. There were replicas of his botanical gardens, paintings (including a copy of the Mona Lisa), and even his personal quarters—his bedroom, kitchen, study, and chapel.

This experience was a bucket list-worthy stop, and I highly recommend it to anyone with an interest in history, aviation, or engineering.

Flying for this benevolent and gracious family was an honor and a privilege, making for some of the most rewarding years of my career.

30
FLIGHT 30R

I have been incredibly grateful to serve what I consider my extended family—the "Sails in Concert" crew—for such a long period of time. During my tenure with Jimmy Buffett's production group, I became aware of JB's extensive philanthropy, but it wasn't until after his passing that I truly grasped the depth and impact of his charitable reach.

A portion of every concert ticket went toward numerous charities, supporting a vast range of causes. To quote JB himself:

"Have Fun, Make Money, and Leave the World a Better Place."

It seems only fitting to recognize just a partial list of the incredible causes that benefited from Jimmy Buffett's generosity:

- Singing for a Change
- Save the Manatee
- Precious Paws
- Wounded Warrior and Freedom Fighters
- Reef Relief
- Jerry Garcia Foundation
- Quiksilver Foundation
- Sweet Relief Musicians Fund
- Gulf Specimen Marine Laboratory
- MD Anderson Cancer Center

- Mary Philanthropy Projects
- Glide Foundation

His philanthropy spanned the entire spectrum—supporting animals, conservation, creative arts, business and economic development, environmental protection, hunger relief, ocean conservation, peace initiatives, employment support, and veteran services.

GITMO

JB had a particularly strong connection with the U.S. military, especially the Navy and Marines. He performed on aircraft carriers, bases, and military facilities across the globe, always giving back to those who served.

One particularly memorable trip was when we flew JB and his BEACH band (JB, Ralph MacDonald, and Mac McAnally) to Naval Base Guantanamo Bay (Gitmo) to entertain the guards and administrative personnel stationed there.

HIDDEN RUNWAYS • 135

One of JB's most cherished partnerships was with "Freedom Fighters Outdoors," founded by Captain Vinny and Sarah LaSorsa of Last Mango Boatworks fame.

My son Marc, along with his co-pilot (his mom!), proudly supported Freedom Fighters, flying veterans to events sponsored by JB's Last Mango organization

My son, Marc, taking off in his Beechcraft Bonanza from Montauk to pick up a group of Freedom Fighters in Philadelphia.

Every New Year, Captain Vinnie would organize a gathering of injured veterans in Montauk, Long Island for a weekend of food, fishing, and camaraderie. Volunteers provided transportation, fishing boats, and meals, creating a truly special experience for the veterans.

These Freedom Fighter gatherings became a "Happy Place" for those who attended. Occasionally, JB would show up unexpectedly, simply to shake hands with as many veterans as possible —a true testament to his genuine heart and appreciation for those who served.

A joyful group of Freedom Fighters joins in on "Fins to the Left, Fins to the Right." Photo credit: Vinnie LaSorsa

Jimmy Buffett's legacy isn't just about music, Margaritaville, or the concerts—it's about the lives he touched, the hands he shook, and the difference he made in the world.

31

FLIGHT 31L

Photo courtesy of Chris Dixon.

For me, "Lone Palm Tree" has a special meaning. On one of our *Continental Drifter 2* "Choey Lee Yacht Shadowing" missions, Ralph Knight and I were assigned while Jimmy was sailing in the San Blas Archipelagoes region off the coast of Central America. When Jimmy and family had completed their activities for the day, we had to find a proper place to "tie down" our Amphibian Caravan for an overnight stay. And there it was—the perfect spot: a very small, unnamed island just big enough to nourish a singular "Lone Palm" and strong enough to hold down our "strange bird" during occasional gusts, by securing it with knots above the "Boy Scout" merit badge level and tie-down procedures that only Ralph was aware of—and considered all part of his seaplane pilot repertoire. He was an excellent seaplane pilot. Of course, neither one of us had a camera to catalogue this event!

Admiral "Red" Best, who played a crucial role in helping JB establish "Air Margaritaville" flight operations, gave an incredibly moving interview on November 4, 2023, reflecting on his 30-year relationship with Jimmy Buffett. Admiral Best spoke passionately about Jimmy's deep love for the military, especially the U.S. Navy.

JB often referred to him as "Redman", and it was Best who introduced the term "Bubbles Up", which JB later immortalized in song. The Admiral also gave JB his Navy call sign, "Brillo", and helped lay the foundation for JB's Air Menagerie in the 1990s. His "Chaos Control" manual became an essential tool for managing unforeseen challenges, supplementing our Flight Operations and General Administrative Manuals. It was a resource I turned to many times as Managing Director and Chief Pilot.

To hear Admiral Best's heartfelt interview, visit the following link:

https://fb.watch/o3L8wjCOs5/?mibextid=SphRi8

In 2003, Jimmy once again demonstrated his incredible business acumen. When Seagram's Whiskey and Liquor Division (which produced Margaritaville Imported Tequila) was sold to the French company Vivendi, JB discovered that his crown jewel —the Hemisphere Dancer—was not included in the deal.

This iconic amphibious aircraft, with "Margaritaville Imported" proudly painted on the underside of the wings, was an integral part of Jimmy's brand. However, Seagram's refused to allow the Hemisphere Dancer to be part of the transaction.

Determined to keep it, JB asked his team to find a solution, ideally one that involved a third-party purchase.

As part of my due diligence, I contacted the Consul General of Kiribati, an island nation about 1,200 miles south of Hawaii, to see if they were interested in using the HD as a transport plane for sports fishermen visiting their world-renowned bone fishing waters—a favorite fishing hole for JB himself.

It could also serve as a critical medivac aircraft for medical emergencies. After reviewing operating costs and maintenance requirements, the Kiribati government passed on the opportunity.

Jimmy turned to his business team for alternatives, but none were particularly viable—until someone (I don't recall who) came up with an idea that caught JB's attention:

Why not turn the Hemisphere Dancer into a restaurant?

At first, the concept seemed impractical. The aircraft's cabin was too small to accommodate enough tables to generate a profit, even with multiple seatings per day. But then, someone proposed an idea that made perfect sense—make the Hemisphere Dancer the centerpiece of a companion restaurant near Margaritaville at Universal Studios CityWalk in Orlando, Florida.

The concept was approved, and the order was given to Craig Young (Chief Pilot of Mirabella Yachts Aviation) and John Stephenson (his co-captain and mechanic) to deliver the Hemisphere Dancer from Fort Pierce (KFPR) to New Smyrna Beach Airport (KEVB) for dismantling and transport to Universal Studios.

Craig and John did not take this mission lightly. It was a sad journey, knowing this was the final flight for a plane that had meant so much to JB and the Margaritaville family. Some avionics, like the radar and GPS, were removed, but the rest of the aircraft remained intact for its transformation.

The Hemisphere Dancer found its new home at the Lone Palm Airport, where it became an instant success. Fans could now experience the magic of JB's legendary seaplane, which continues to be a beloved part of his legacy.

The keys to the aircraft were handed over to Jennifer Lebono and Sherri Young, who became its official caretakers. Dan

Leonard and Jonathan Cohlan ensured that the transition was handled with the respect and reverence the aircraft deserved.

Since its arrival, the Hemisphere Dancer has become a huge attraction, drawing fans from all over to relive the adventures and spirit of Jimmy Buffett.

Above all, this journey wasn't just about moving an airplane—it was about preserving a piece of JB's heart and soul, ensuring that his legacy would continue to inspire Parrot Heads for generations to come.

Above - Last Day for Two "Strange Birds" Before They Fly to Their New Nest!

All good things must come to an end—two "Strange Birds" are waiting on the PBI ramp, ready to fly off to their new nest. A bittersweet day for all of us who were part of Air Margaritaville.

In 1997, a "Cat Event" unfolded during one of our annual repositioning trips to the USA—first to Oxnard, California, and then on to Tucson, Arizona, for our annual maintenance inspection on our CL-600 Challenger at the Bombardier Service Center.

Shortly after departing Berlin, during the climb toward Reykjavik, Iceland, for a technical (fuel) stop, a loud, single *bang*—like a cannon blast—grabbed our immediate attention. After scanning everything in the cockpit, we noticed a vertical crack on the left-hand (pilot's side) windshield. It stretched from the top to the bottom of the windshield's outer glass panel.

We immediately leveled off and contacted Prestwick ATC to declare an emergency. The nearest, most suitable emergency airport was Prestwick, Scotland. ATC approved our request to change course to EGPK (Glasgow Prestwick Airport).

We referred to our abnormal and emergency checklists for guidance on a "cracked outer windshield" and began a controlled descent with reduced airspeed and a slower cabin pressure rate toward EGPK.

Shortly after establishing this descent profile, the wife of our senior passenger approached the cockpit. She'd noticed on the "Airshow" screen (which displays flight progress) that we were no longer headed toward Iceland. She asked why we'd changed course, and I briefly explained that we were making a precautionary landing in Prestwick and suggested she return to her seat, perhaps with a cup of tea, while we focused on addressing the situation.

Ten minutes later, she returned—this time with more urgency—demanding to know why we'd diverted. Jamie and I were deep in handling the situation, but I pointed to the cracked windshield and said, "See that crack? If the outer panel separates and glass fragments hit the engines before we reach the airport, we might have to ditch in the freezing Atlantic Ocean. Jamie and I are working hard to prevent that from happening. I strongly recommend you return to your seat, tighten your seatbelt, and let us do our job of getting everyone safely on the ground."

That got her attention. She returned to her seat immediately.

We landed safely at EGPK, but what happened next was something we hadn't anticipated.

Scottish Customs and Immigration officers boarded the aircraft after it was declared safe. Unbeknownst to us, they requested documentation for our passengers' cats—shot records, health certificates—anything that confirmed the cats weren't carrying diseases or other health concerns.

When the officers informed the passengers that the cats would need to remain in Prestwick for a legally required six-month quarantine, the wife burst into tears. I stepped in to calm the situation and offered a solution: I suggested that while we ferried the aircraft to London for windshield repairs, the cats could be transported to a licensed quarantine facility via a bonded ambulance. They would stay there until our repairs were complete and receive full health exams, with proper paperwork in place for the onward journey to the USA. Thankfully, both the officials and the cat owners agreed.

With that crisis resolved, we turned our attention to ferrying the aircraft to London. Replacing the left-hand windshield presented a fresh set of challenges. The extreme cold—Europe's coldest temperatures in years—meant we had to find a hangar with an ambient temperature high enough for the windshield sealant to cure properly, as specified in Bombardier's maintenance manual.

After consulting with the manufacturer, we were authorized to fly at low altitude, below 10,000 feet, at reduced speed, staying clear of clouds and any IFR (Instrument Flight Rules) conditions along the way.

The manufacturer processed our ferry permit, and off we went to EGLL (Heathrow Airport), where the Harrods FBO hangar could meet the necessary temperature requirements.

Before departing Prestwick, we applied 3M Metal Foil Adhesive Tape (425-DWB 10193-02) over the full length of the crack to prevent any separation of the windshield's outer panel. Luckily, the EGPK airport had the tape in stock, which expedited our low-and-slow journey to London.

The flight itself was fascinating. We passed several abandoned airfields used by B-17 crews during World War II—a humbling reminder of history.

With the frigid temperatures, replacing the windshield took over a week. As for the cats? The cost of their "maintenance" was astronomical, but the owner didn't complain once. In the end, all seemed well—until we discovered that only one cat returned with us on the trip back to Berlin. Unfortunately, the other had been deemed unfit for travel due to health concerns.

This "Cat Event" taught us an unforgettable lesson about transporting animals across international borders—always be prepared, and make sure the cats don't have their own emergency landing of sorts.

32

LASTLY, A FEW WORDS OF WISDOM FROM JIMMY BUFFETT

"It takes no more time to see the good side of life than to see the bad."

"I have always looked at life as a voyage—mostly wonderful, sometimes frightening. In my family and friends, I have discovered treasure more valuable than gold."

"Grief is like the wake behind a boat. It starts as a huge wave, following close behind, big enough to swamp and drown you if you suddenly stop moving forward. But if you keep going, the big wake will eventually dissipate. And after a long time, the waters of your life grow calm again—that's when the memories of those we've lost begin to shine as bright and enduring as the stars above."

"Go fast enough to get there, but slow enough to see."

"Be yourself, be pleasant, play hard, and have no regrets."

"Therapy is extremely expensive. Popping bubble wrap is radically cheap."

"Some make the world go 'round; others watch it turn."

"Fun is about as good a habit as there is."

"Is it ignorance or apathy? Hey, I don't know, and I don't care."

"It's important to have as much fun as possible while we're here. It balances out the times when the minefield of life explodes."

"Later down the road of life, I discovered that salt water is also good for the mental abrasions one inevitably acquires on land."

"Searching is half the fun—life is much more manageable when thought of as a scavenger hunt rather than a surprise party."

"Whether it's a letter, song lyrics, part of a novel, or instructions on how to fix a kitchen sink, it's writing. You keep your craft honed, you acquire the discipline to finish things, and you turn into a self-taskmaster."

THE END!

*Off to Margaritaville with **Captain Buffett**...*

"Life is a journey that's measured not in miles or year, but in experiences"
— Jimmy Buffett

That's my story... and I'm sticking to it!

ACKNOWLEDGMENTS

This book would not have been possible without the support of those who helped me recall events spanning 50 years. From my childhood, college, military service, consulting career, and Jimmy Buffett tours to my years beyond, I've aimed to provide readers with interesting and factual "back" stories from real sources. Below are the individuals to whom I owe my deepest gratitude for making this book an "open window" into my life as a corporate pilot and employee of one of the most fascinating human beings to ever walk, sail, and fly around this planet—Jimmy Buffett.

WITH DEEPEST APPRECIATION

Mrs. Jane Buffett (and family) – We extend our heartfelt gratitude for your understanding of Jimmy's wish to "keep the party rolling," a sentiment every Parrot Head will surely embrace. On behalf of all Margaritaville believers and participants, we share our love and deepest condolences with the Buffett family.

Mrs. Jane Buffett, thank you for sharing your beautifully written personal note to Jimmy and his fans: ***https://americansongwriter.com/jimmy-buffetts-wife-jane-shares-heartfelt-message-following-husbands-death-thank-you-for-giving-joy-to-him-and-to-me/***

FAMILY & LOVED ONES

- Elli Curreri, my wife of 55 years—your boundless devotion to our family is immeasurable.
- Cristina Curreri, my daughter; Ella and Emily Batogowski, my granddaughters.
- Marc Curreri, my son; Jennifer Curreri, my daughter-in-law; Jackson and Jake Curreri, my grandsons.
- My parents, Vincent and Catherine, and my siblings, Marie, Richard, and David.
- Paul Dardinski, our favorite son-in-law.

AIR MARGARITAVILLE & AVIATION COLLEAGUES

- Billy Schmidt, last Air Margaritaville Flight Department Manager.
- Former Seaplane Pilots: Alex Poulos, Ralph Knight, Bill Howell, Dan Laplace (Supervisor), Warner Boyd (Admin), Steve Tuma, and Gary Roxborough, Master Pilot.
- Greg Evans (and to his father, who founded UV-Air), Ralph Vasami, Joe Rachelle (RET), Lex Den Herder (RET), and the Universal Weather and Aviation Teams, who helped me navigate the planet safely on international trips for over 50 years.
- Dave Hurley, a lifelong friend in aviation.
- Al Ueltschi, Jim Christiansen, Nick Sergi, Don Tilley, Danny Robayo, Captain Ramish Mauley, Bruce Whitman, Jim Waugh, and the FlightSafety training staff.
- Rich Schuller, my friend of over 50 years.
- Greg Alfson, my favorite Norwegian pilot.
- The "Remember Glencar" Falcon 900B Group: Pat Q, Ralph A, Mary B, and John C.
- Mike Wojdylak, Chief Pilot; Chip and DOM Trevor

of John Hendrick's Flight Operation—thank you, John.
- Bob Stangarone, the man who knows everyone in our industry.

MILITARY & SQUADRON MATES

- ADM Bob Dunn and my fellow "Blue Diamond" VA-146 Squadron Mates.
- ADM James "Red" Best, who fostered a wonderful "State of Mind" for us all.
- ADM Mike Bowman and ADM Jones Stanley.
- ADM Bill Harris and Captain Al "S-14" Schaufelberger.
- Captain Eugene "Skip" Crangle, Captain Hugh Loheed, and Captain John "Yams" Yamnicky—Yams, little did I know that 37 years later, you would be a passenger on American Airlines Flight 77, which terrorists flew into the Pentagon. You are forever in my heart.
- Commander Hugh "Slugger" Magee, Commander Carl Niedhold, LCDR "Do Daddy" Dodds, LCDR Bob Kemper, LCDR Charlie Lee, Lieutenant Grant "Peeps" Collier, Lieutenant Bob Reed, Lieutenant James "RAH" Childs, Lieutenant Ralph Larson, and Lieutenant Roger Lawson.
- LT Jeff "Leprechaun" Greedwood, Author of *Jeff's Exploits*, LT Phil "Rags" Ronglien, fellow owner of "Club Shima."

INDUSTRY & ENTERTAINMENT FRIENDS

- Wil Shriner, director of Hoot and son of Herb Shriner.
- Tom Battista, the greatest stage manager and supporter.

- Dr. Les Pickering and Ed Webby, longtime friends.
- Captain Phil, Skipper of Loan Shark, and Diane Johnson.
- Captain Vinnie and Sarah LaSorsa, Last Mango Boatworks and "Freedom Fighters."
- Captain "Spider" Andresen, Marine Margaritaville.
- Captain Richard Allen (USNR), VA-55.
- Gary Roxborough, Master Pilot.
- Greg "Fingers" Taylor.
- Captain Larry "Groovy" Gray, former owner of Air Mango—"Fly Fast, Live Slow."
- Carl Hiaasen, Producer of "Hoot"
- Freedom Fighters Outdoors
- Vinnie and Sarah LaSorsa from Last Mango Boatworks
- Billy Witcher for your generosity
- FBO Managers John Mason, Phil Botana, Jim Mead
- Aircraft Salesmen Bryan Moss, Jerry Smith, Dennis Anderson, (QB) Terry Sherman
- Bill Quinn, Navy Veteran and Aviation Master of all Trades

SPECIAL MENTIONS

- Members of JetFlight Aviation LLC, Flight Operations, Lugano Base.
- Fairwind Charter Operation Pilots.
- Presidential Charter Operations.
- Former Chalks Seaplane Operations (Watson Island, Government Cut, Nassau, Bahamas)—Roger Nair and Bill Jones.
- Captain Craig Young and Captain John Stephenson, Air Margaritaville's seaplane arm, Mirabella Yachts and Hemisphere Dancer Adjunct Flight Operations.
- The MIA/BOS FAA FSDO personnel, for their professionalism, advice, and counsel over the years.

- The outstanding FlightSafety Inc. and CAE training teams.
- Ceasare Baj, for your seaplane wisdom and leadership as Team Manager of Aero Como.
- Tom Evans, Founder of UV-Air Inc.

FOREVER IN MY MEMORIES

Lieutenant Jim "K-12" Knollmueller, Lieutenant Pete "Peanuts" Grubaugh, Lieutenant Larry Collins, Lieutenant Neville Haggerty, LCDR John Baker—you will always be remembered.

To all the thousands of people who took the time and effort to help me along the way—thank you, and God bless you! You know who you are, and I trust, hope, and pray that we'll rendezvous again sometime soon so I can thank you in person.

Bubbles up—and keep the party going!